Welcome to "Feathered Serenity: A Birds Mandala Coloring Book for Adults"!

This book is a celebration of the beauty and diversity of our feathered friends, intricately woven into the spiritual art form of Mandalas. Each page presents a unique Mandala design, featuring different bird species from around the world.

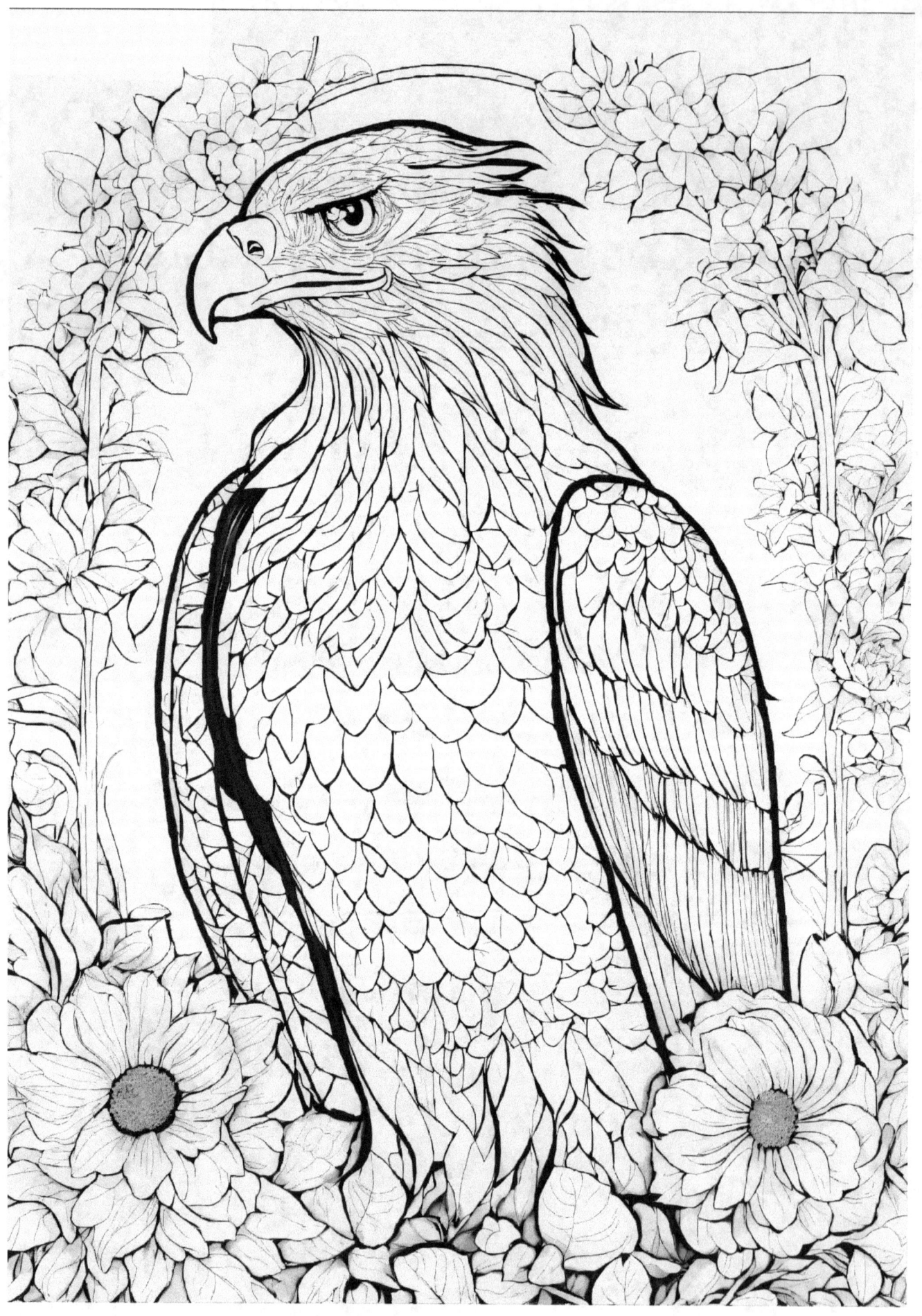

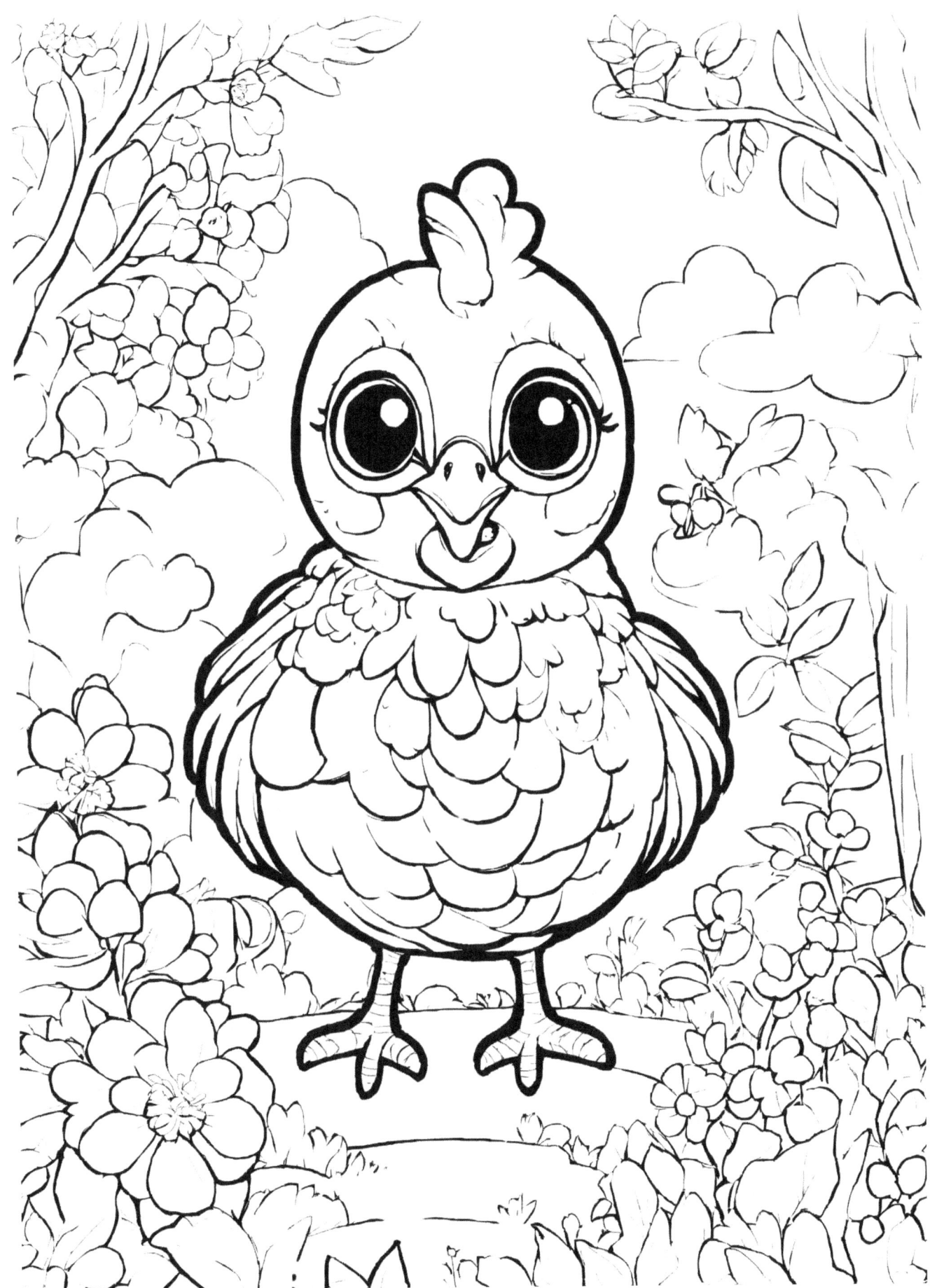

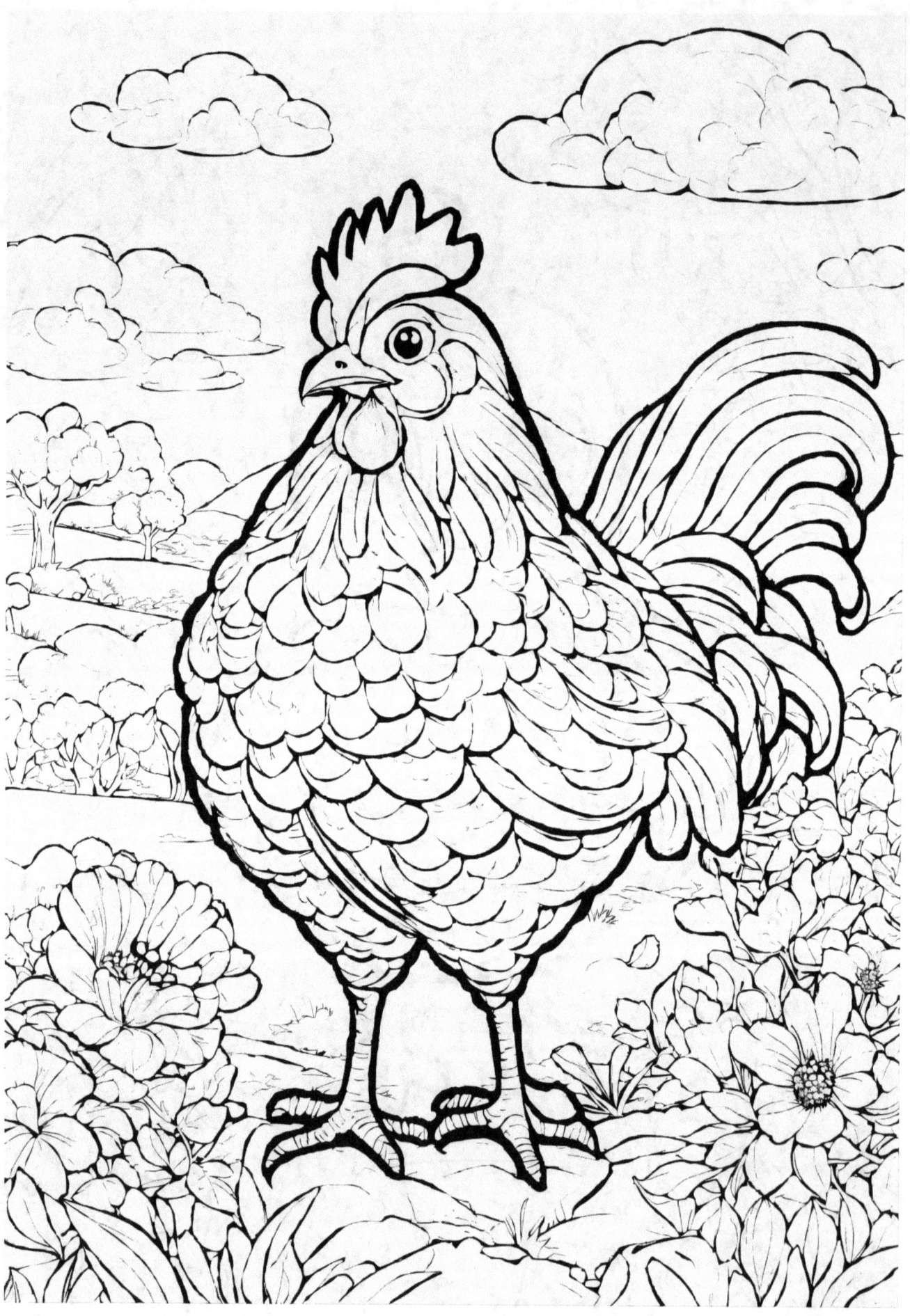

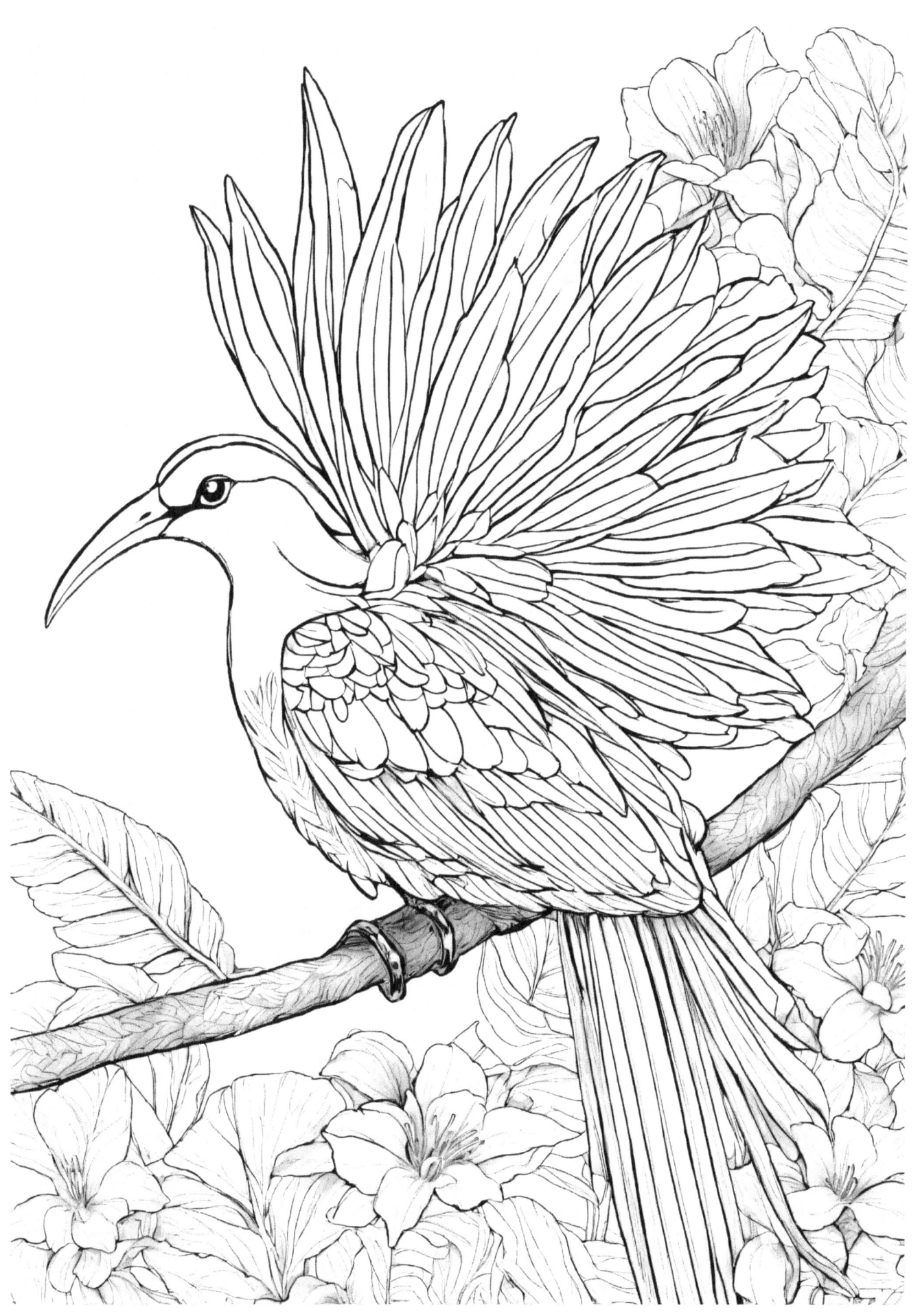

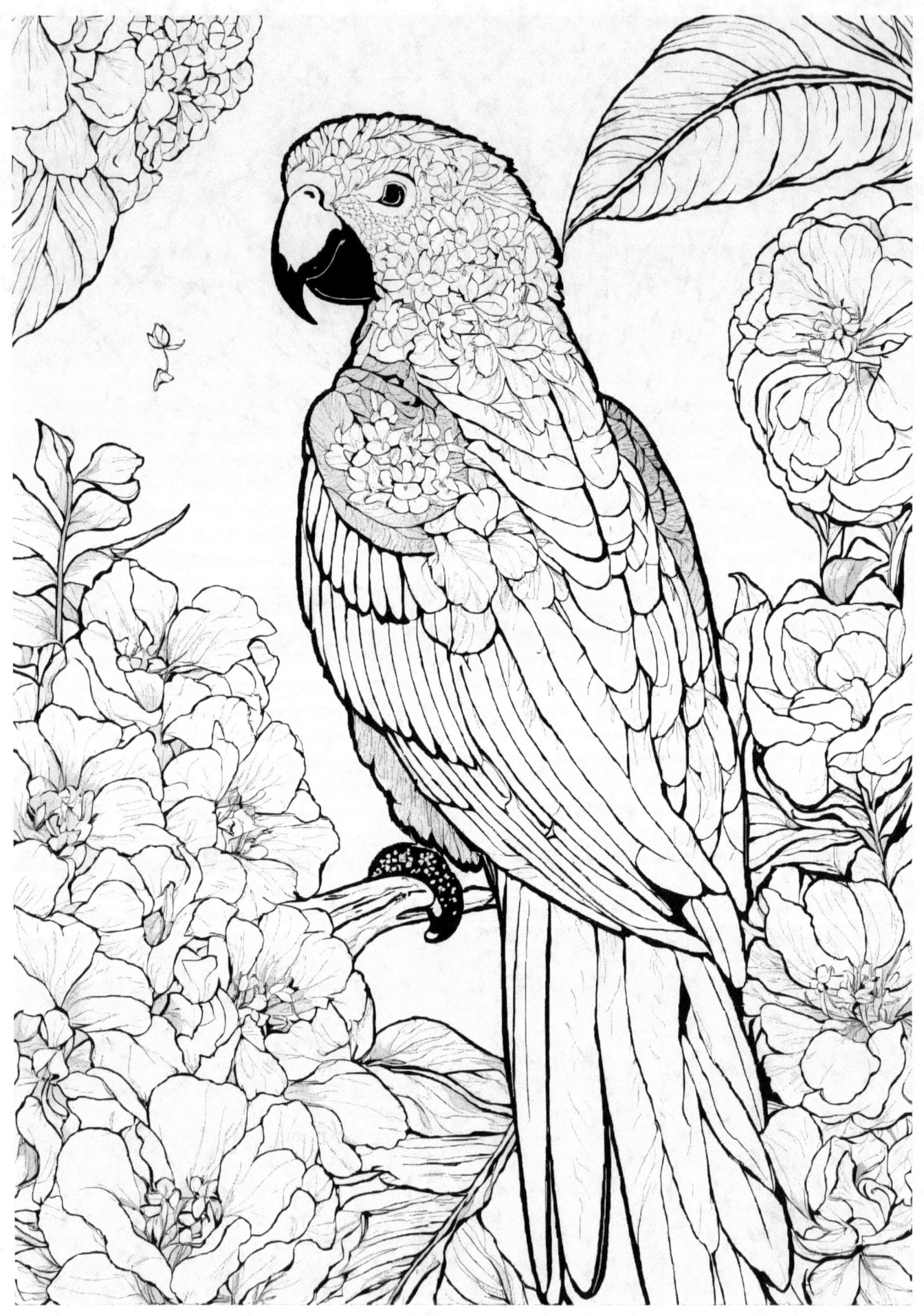

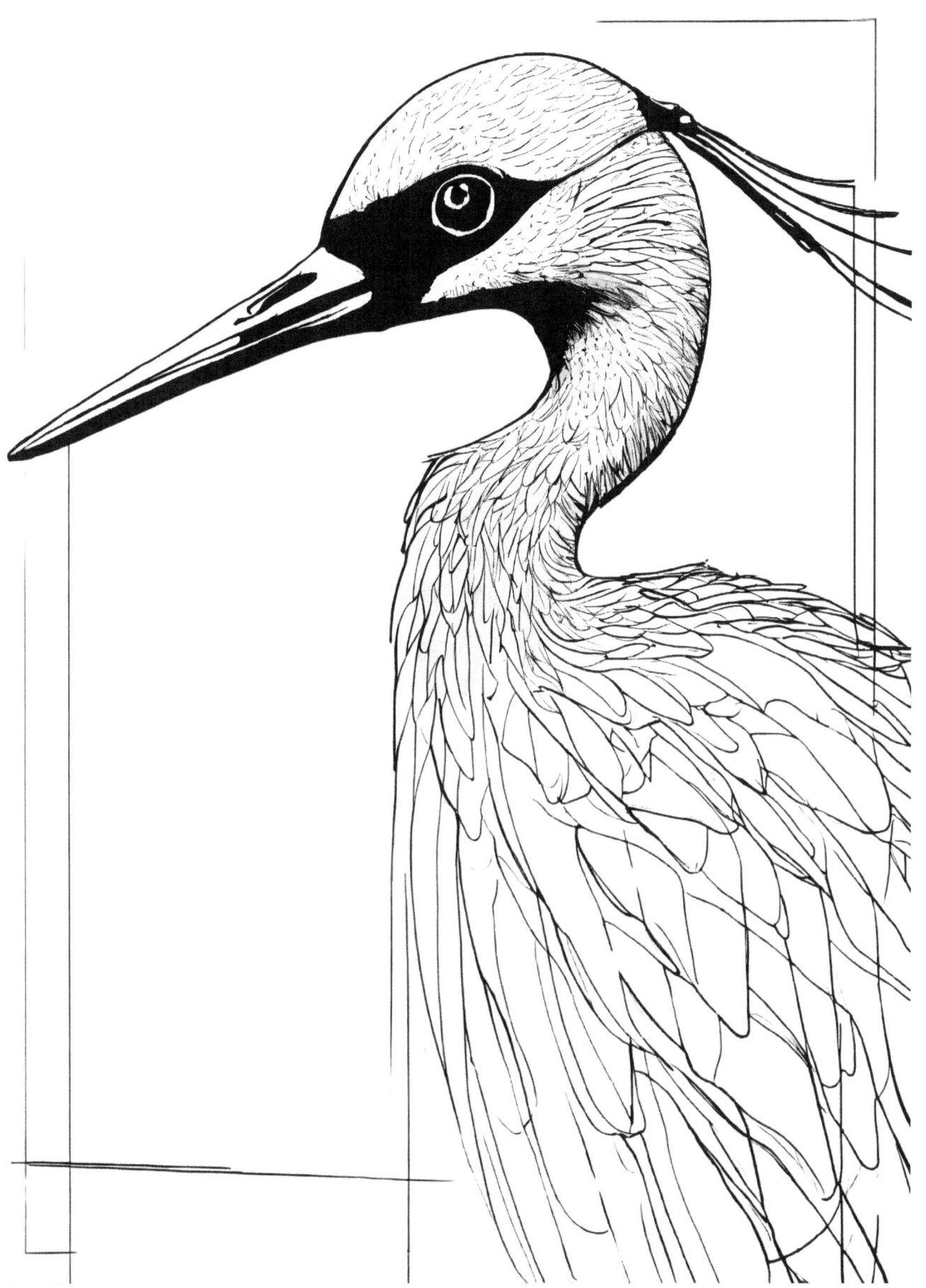

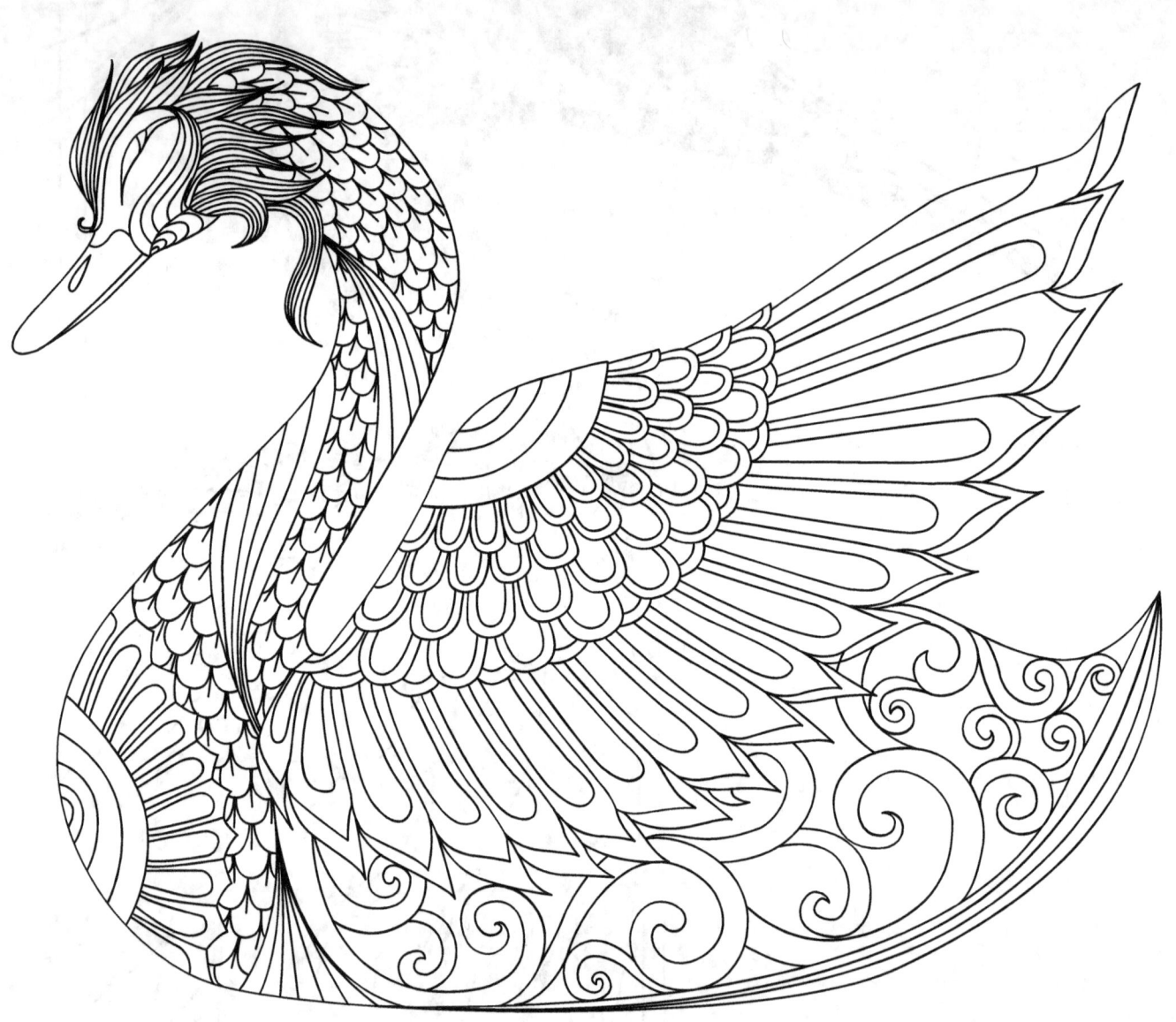

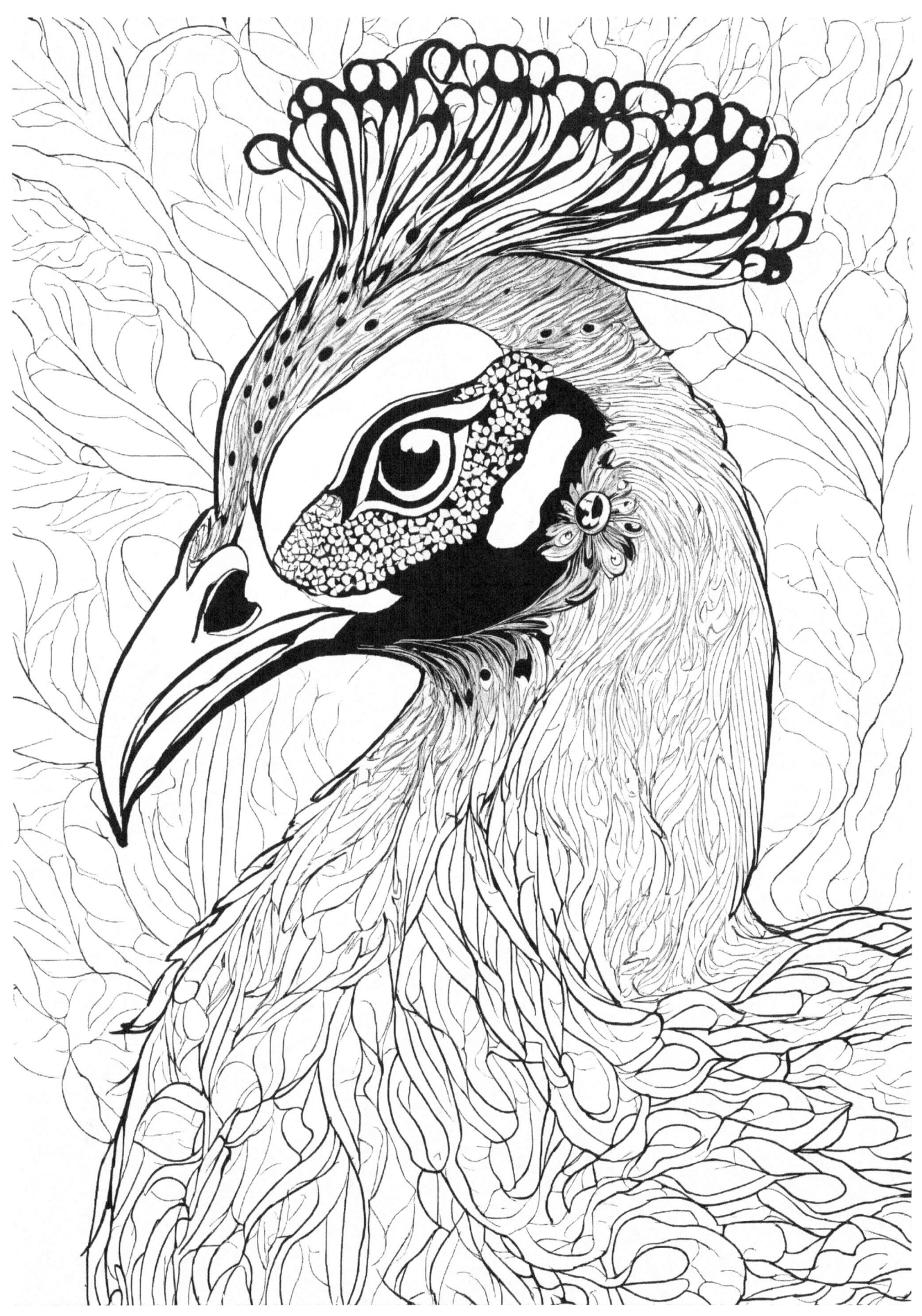

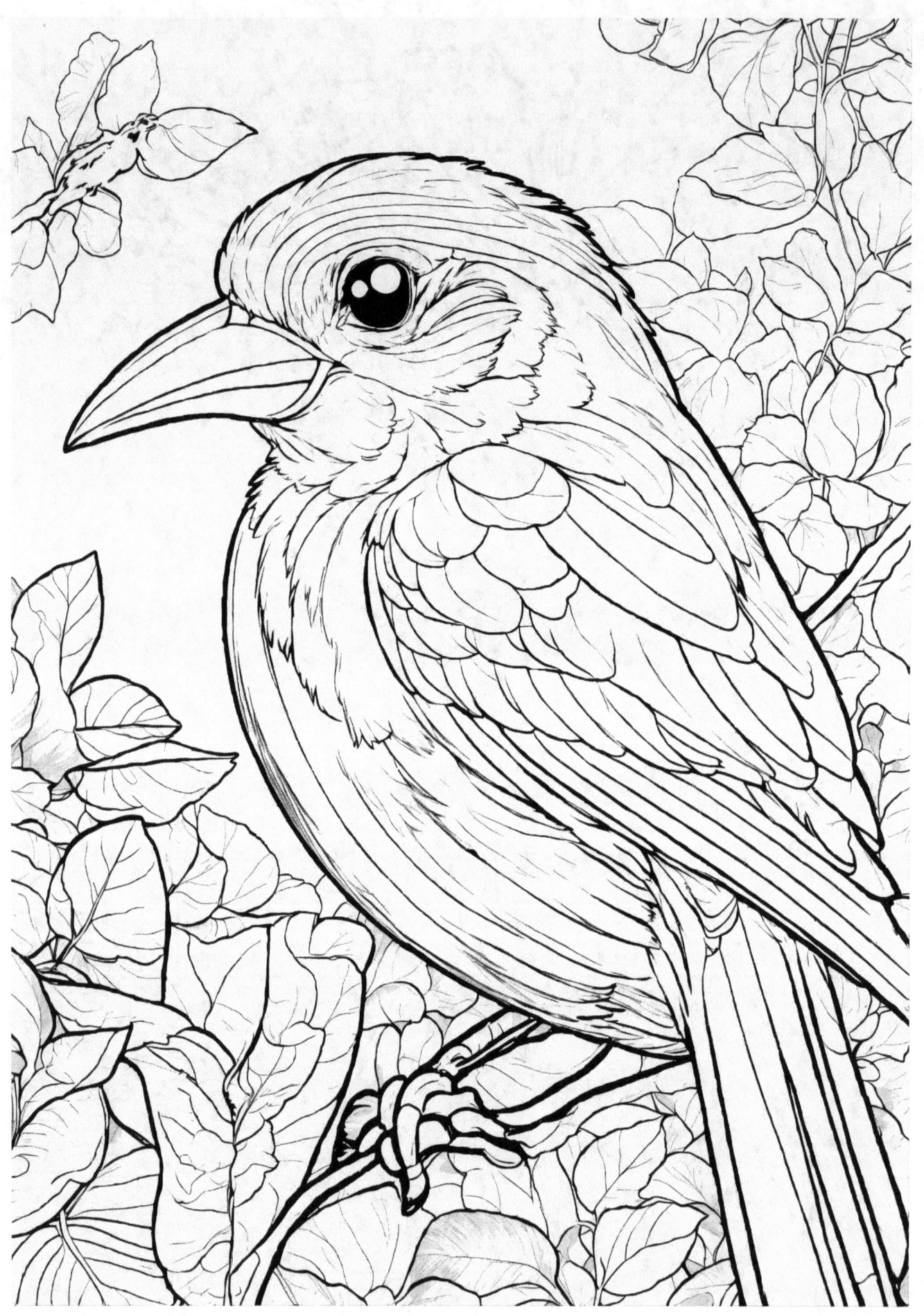

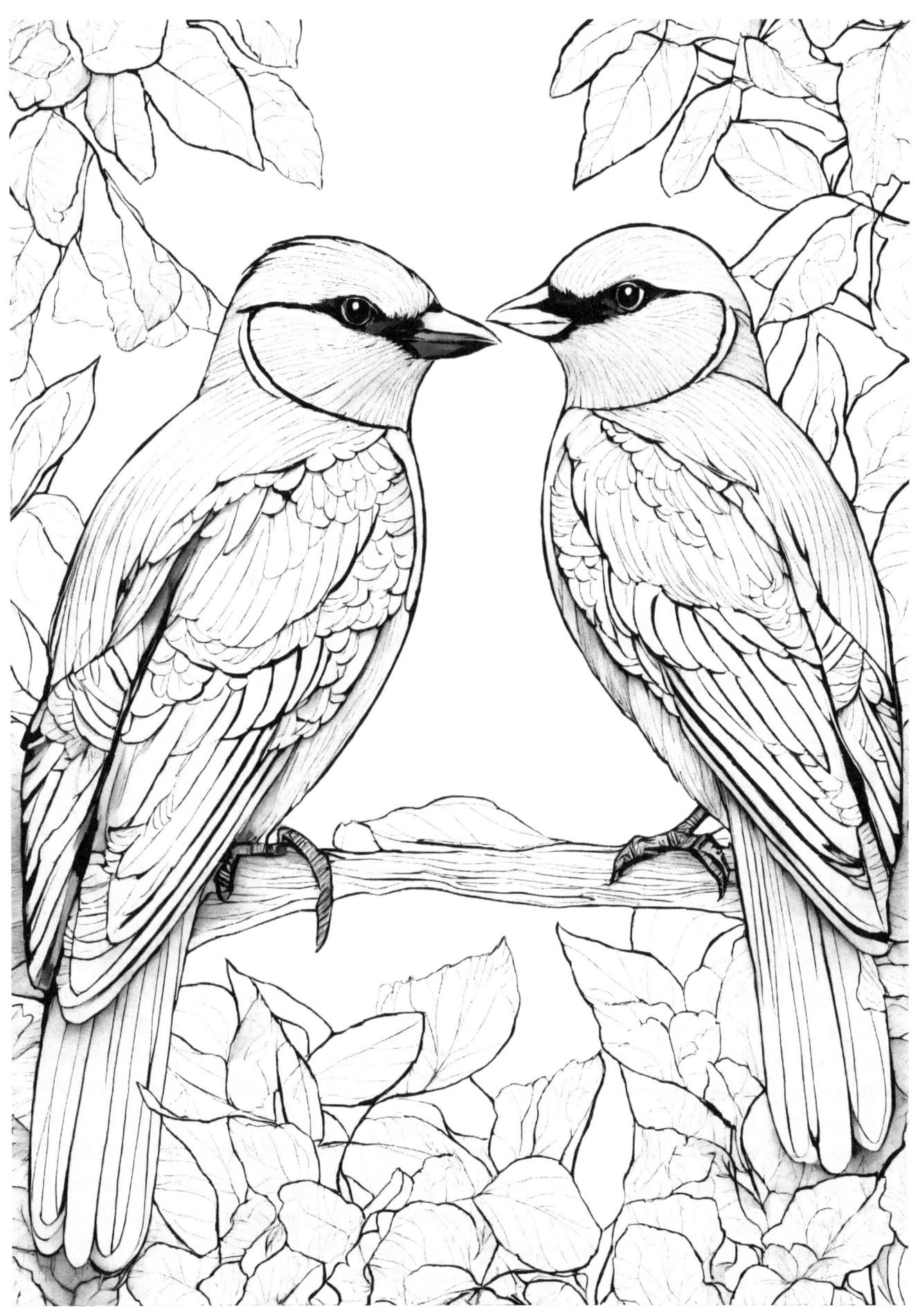

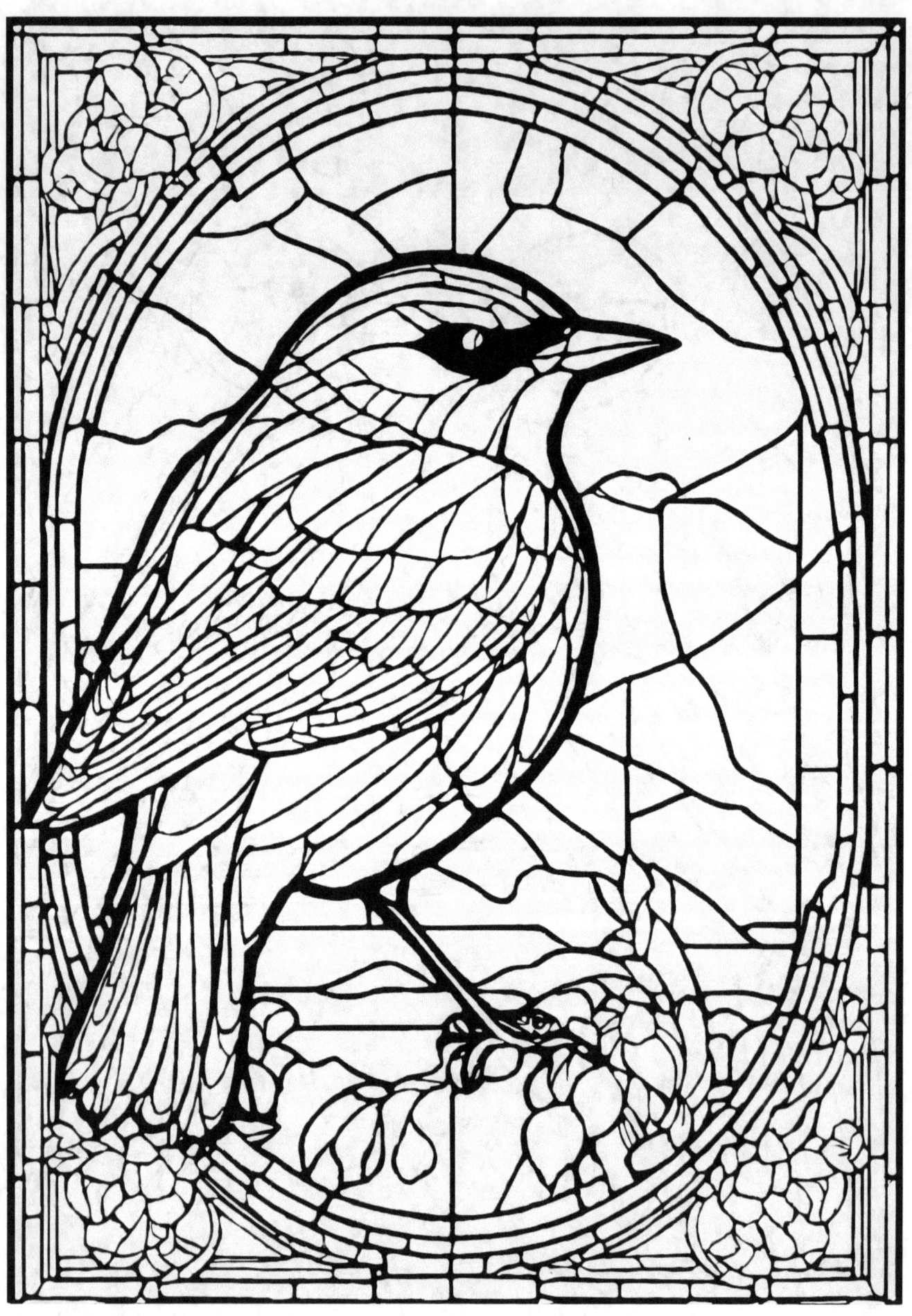

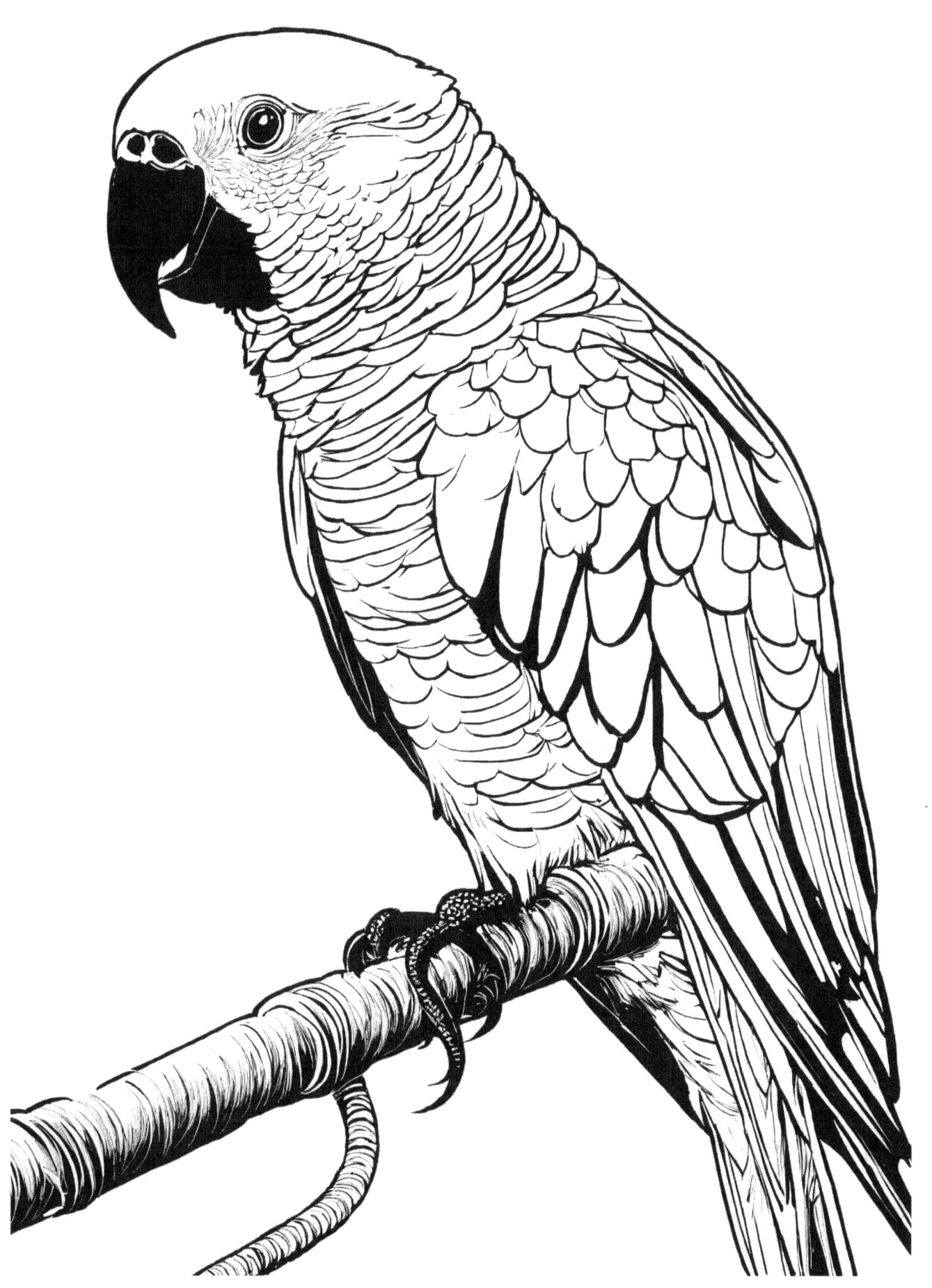

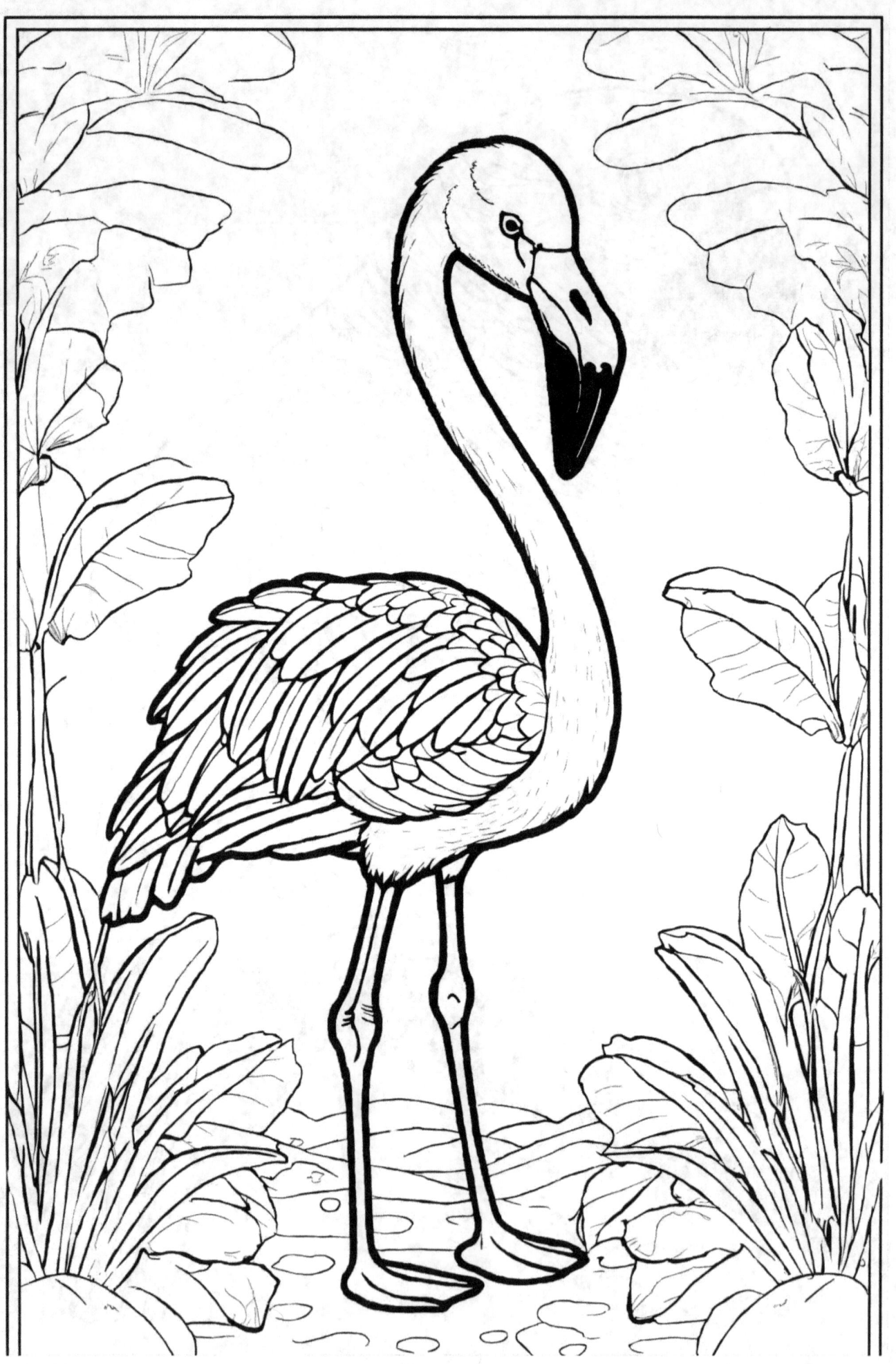

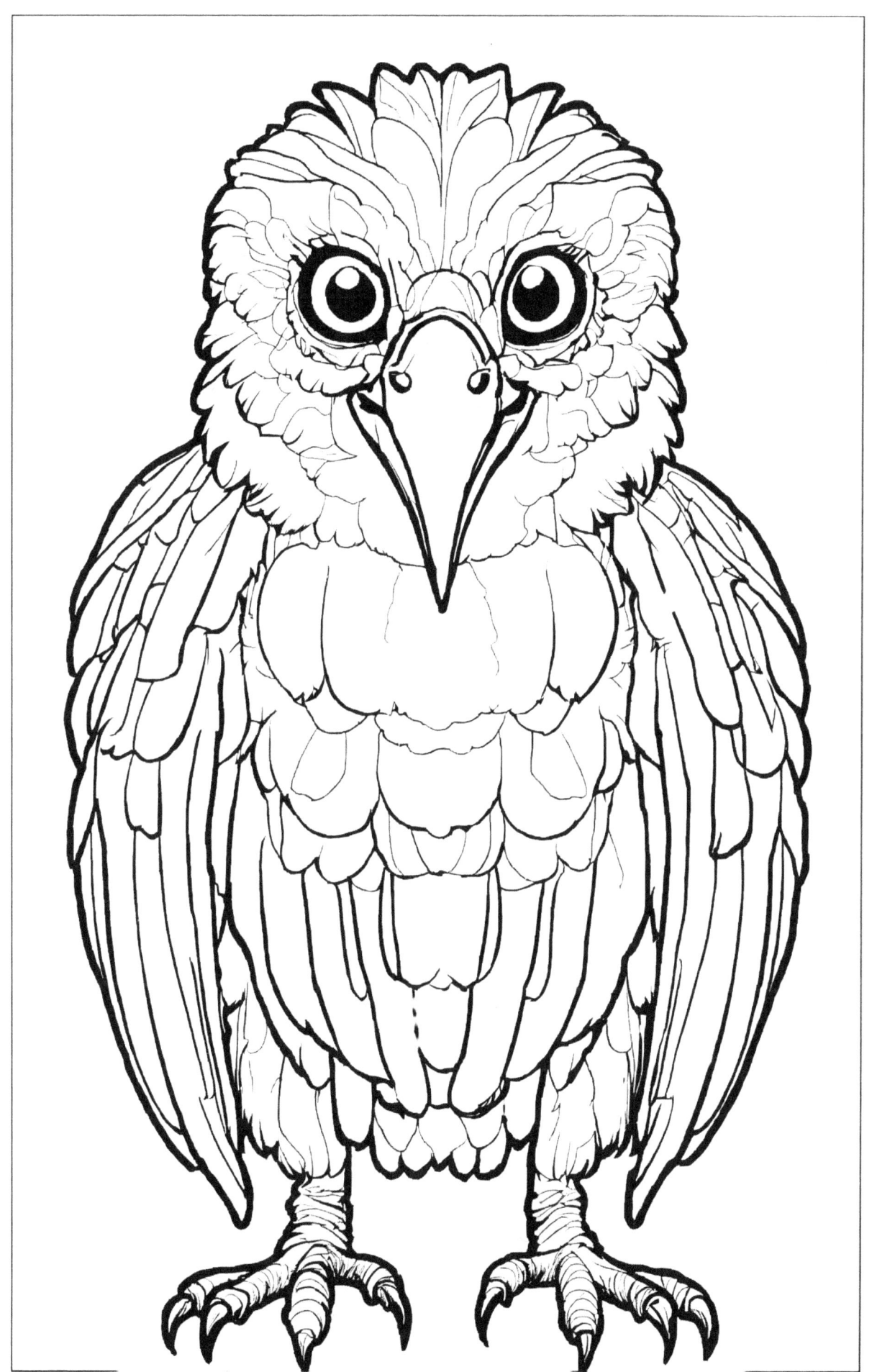

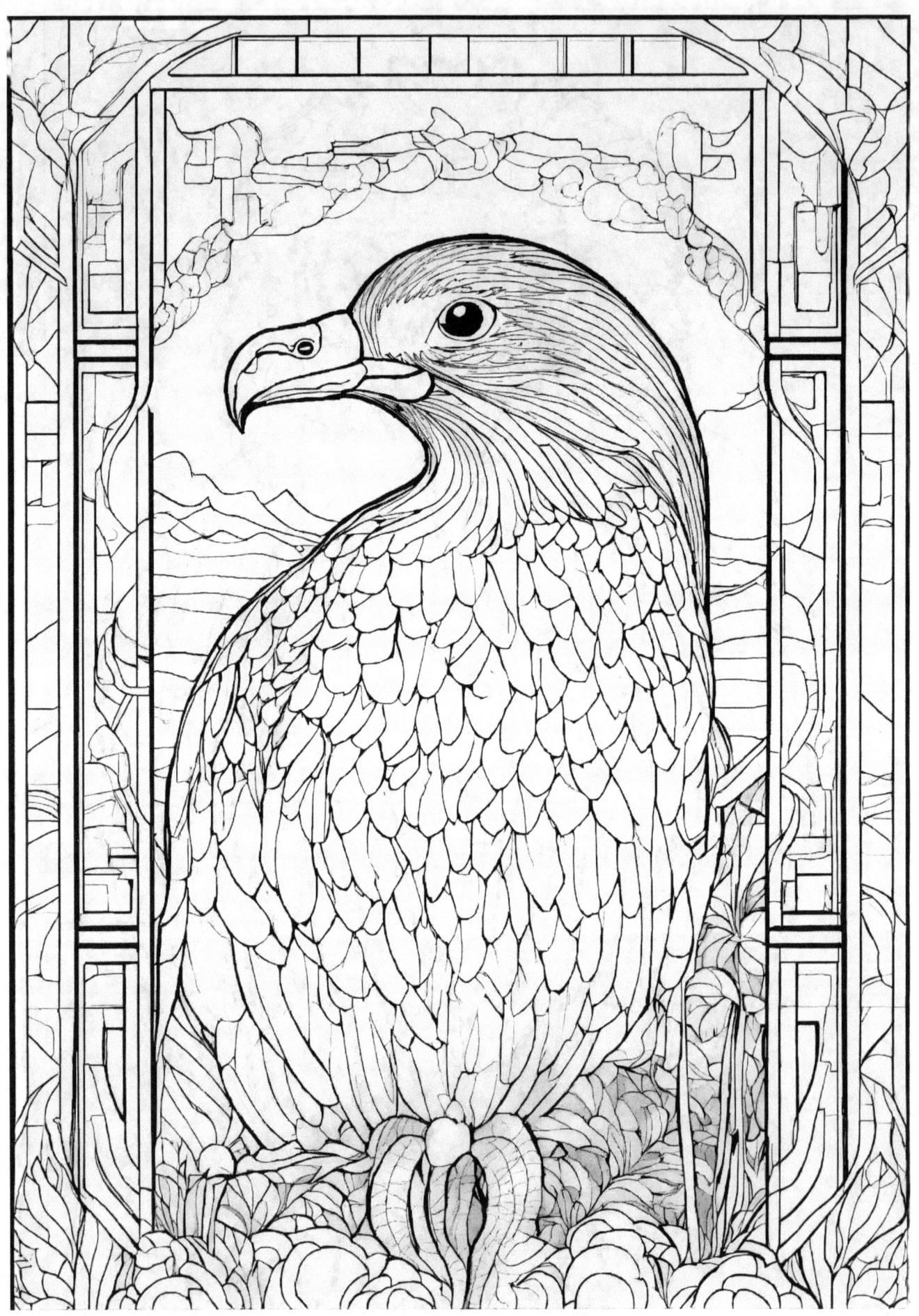

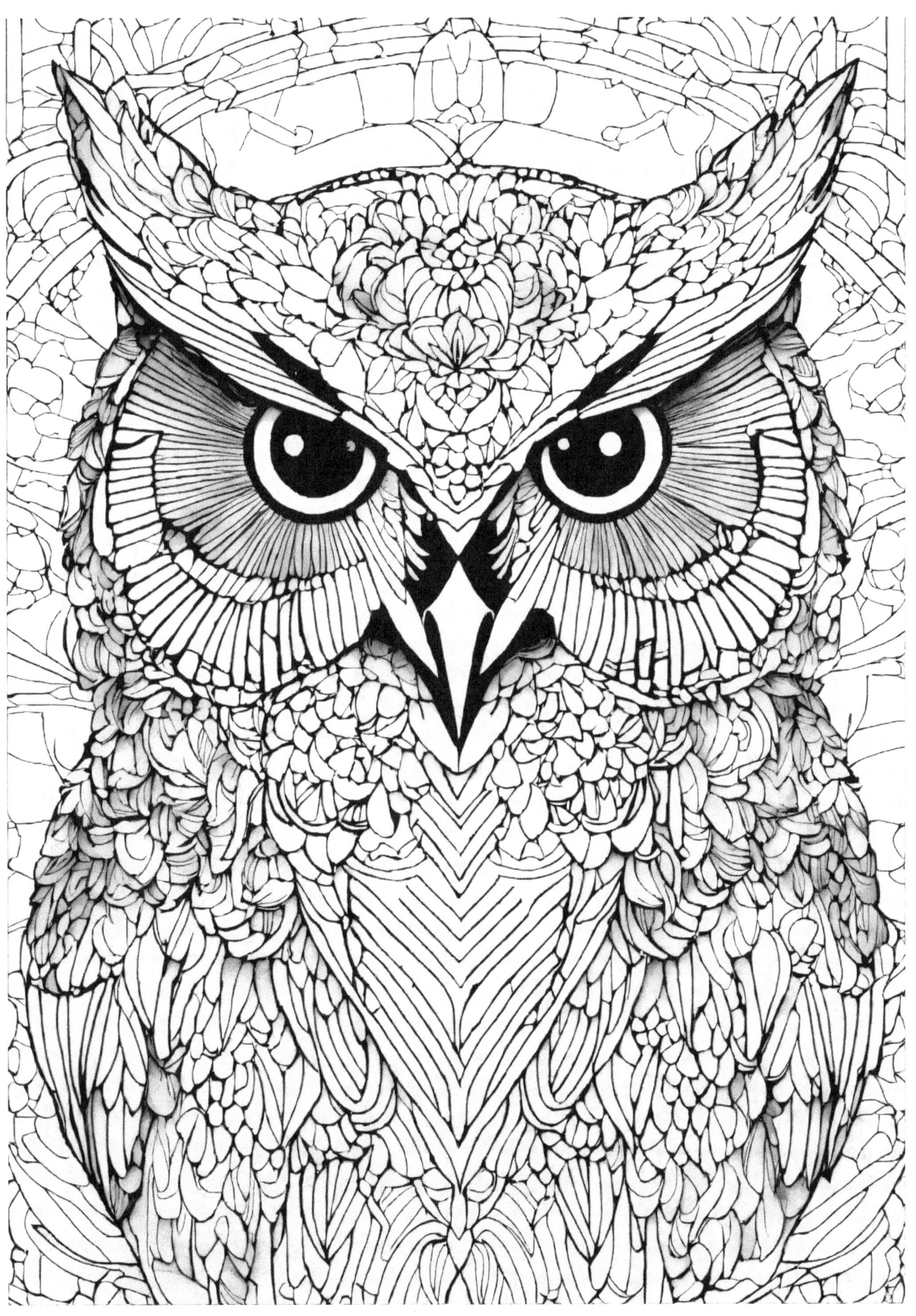

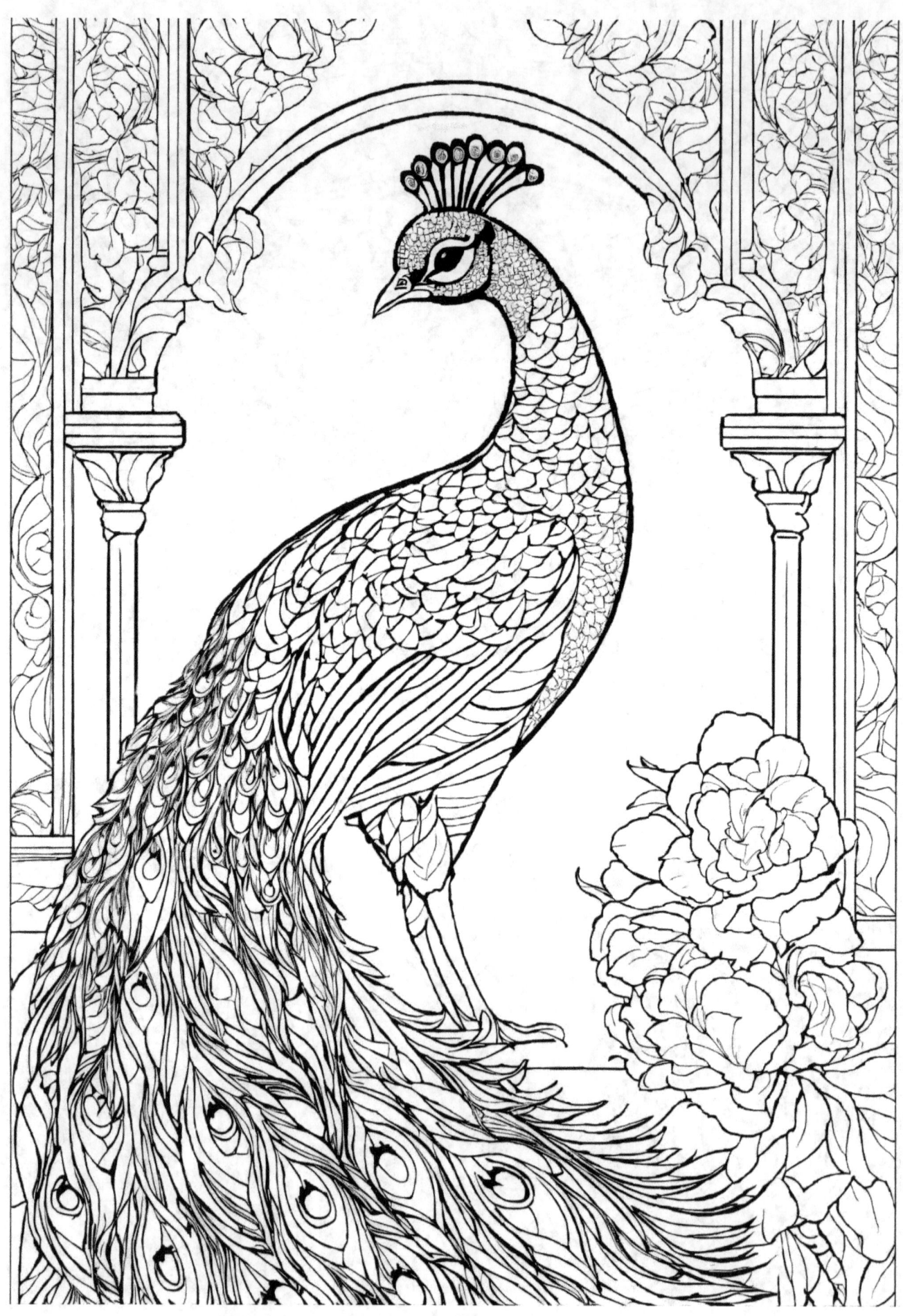

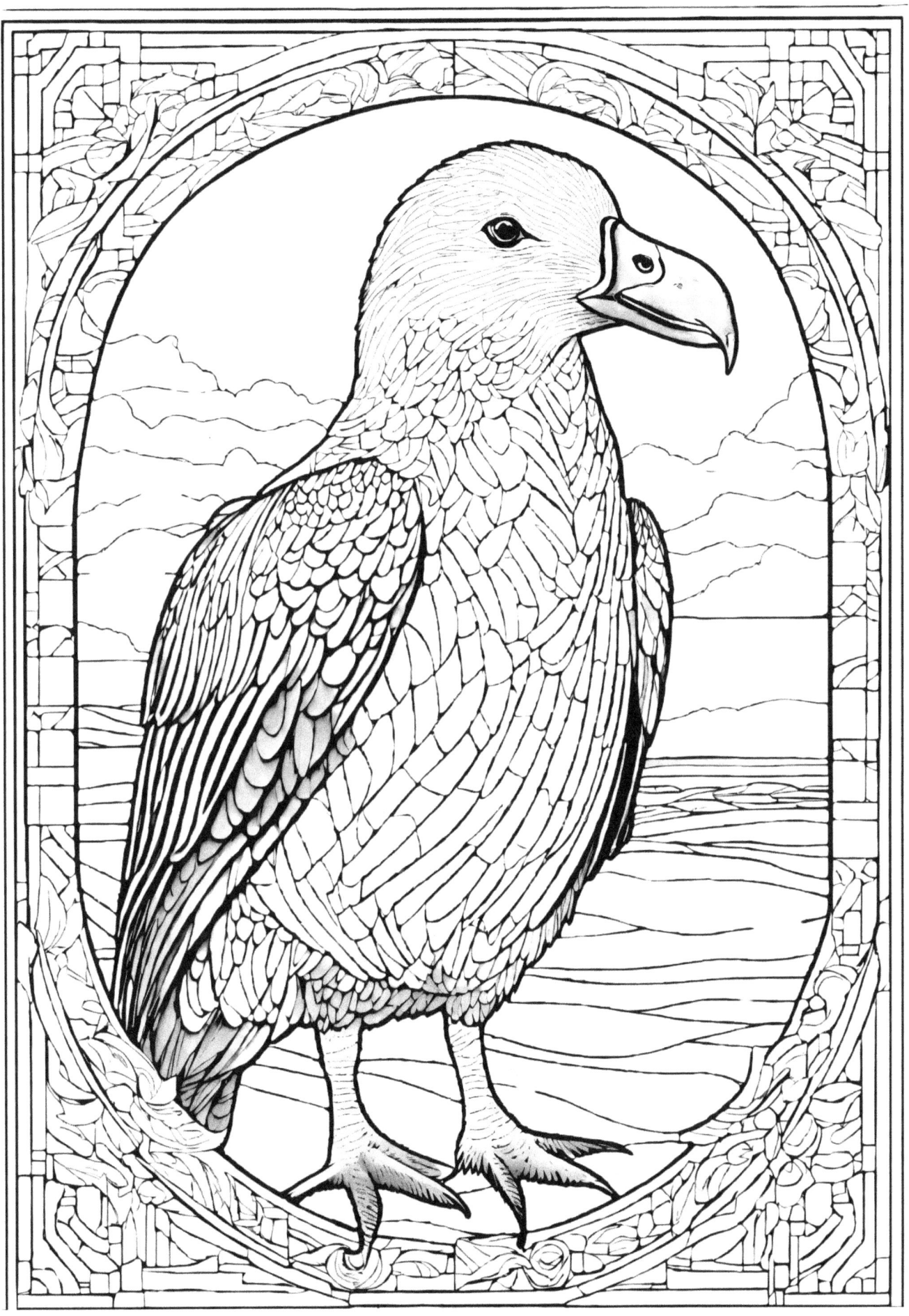

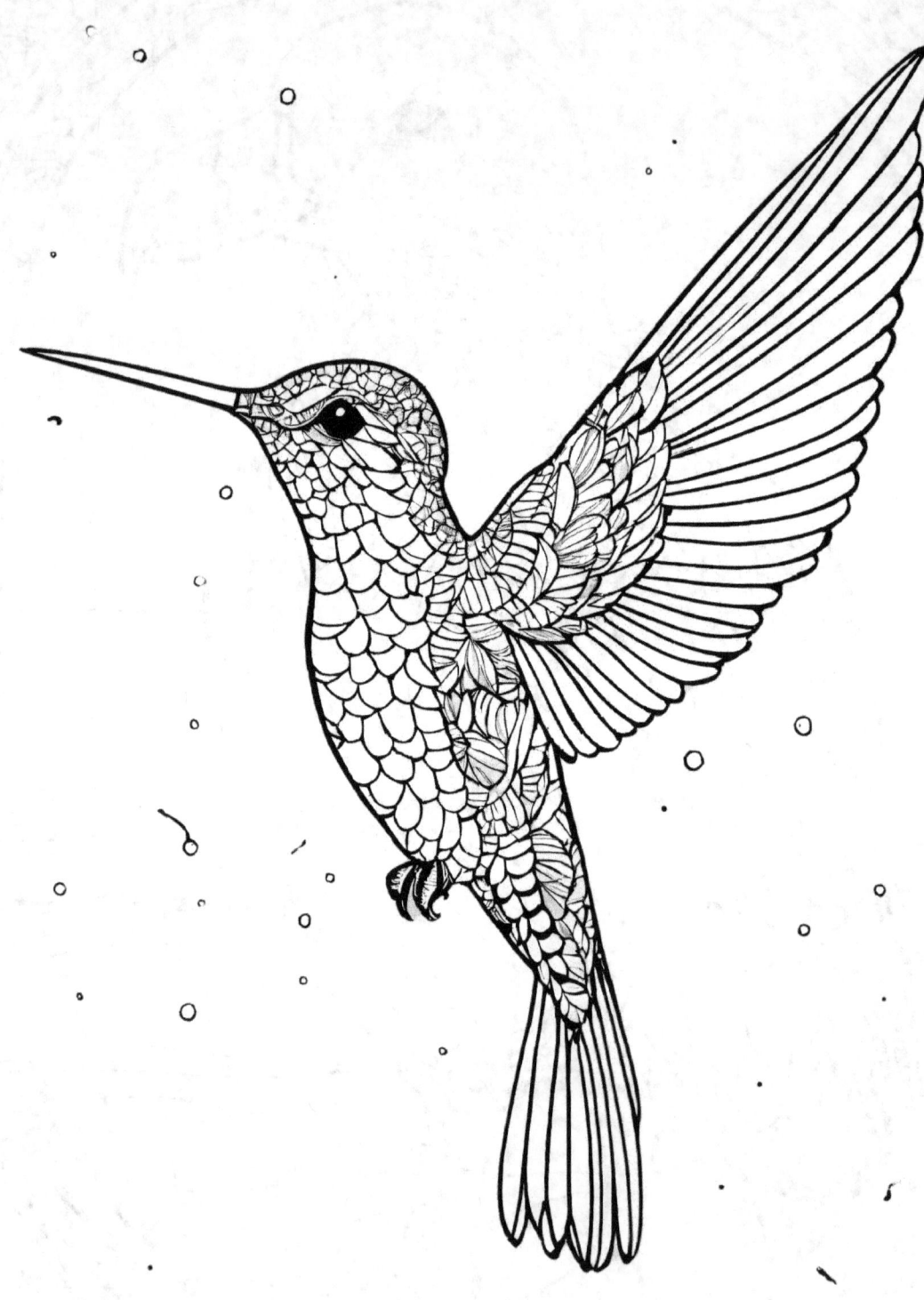

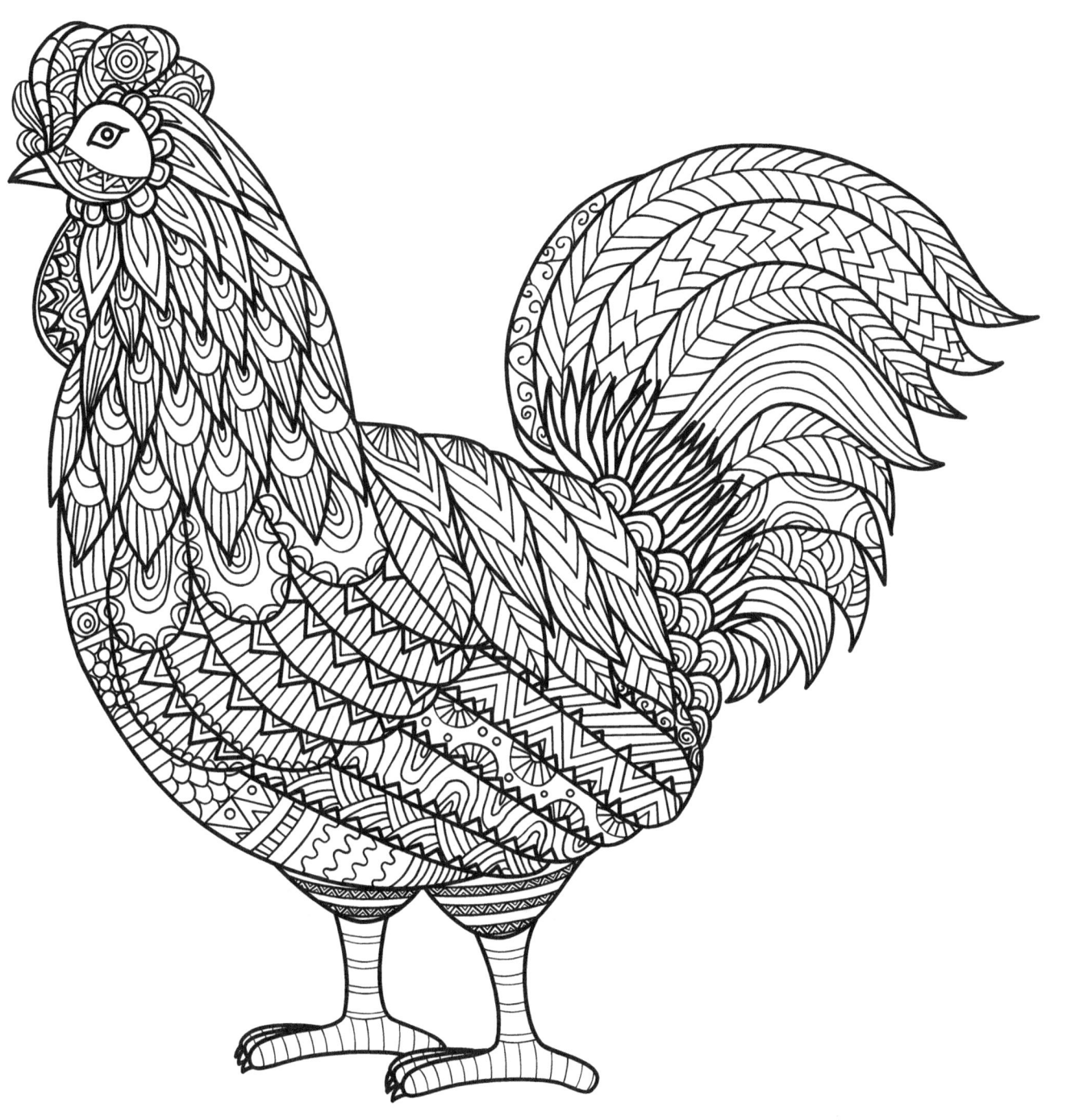

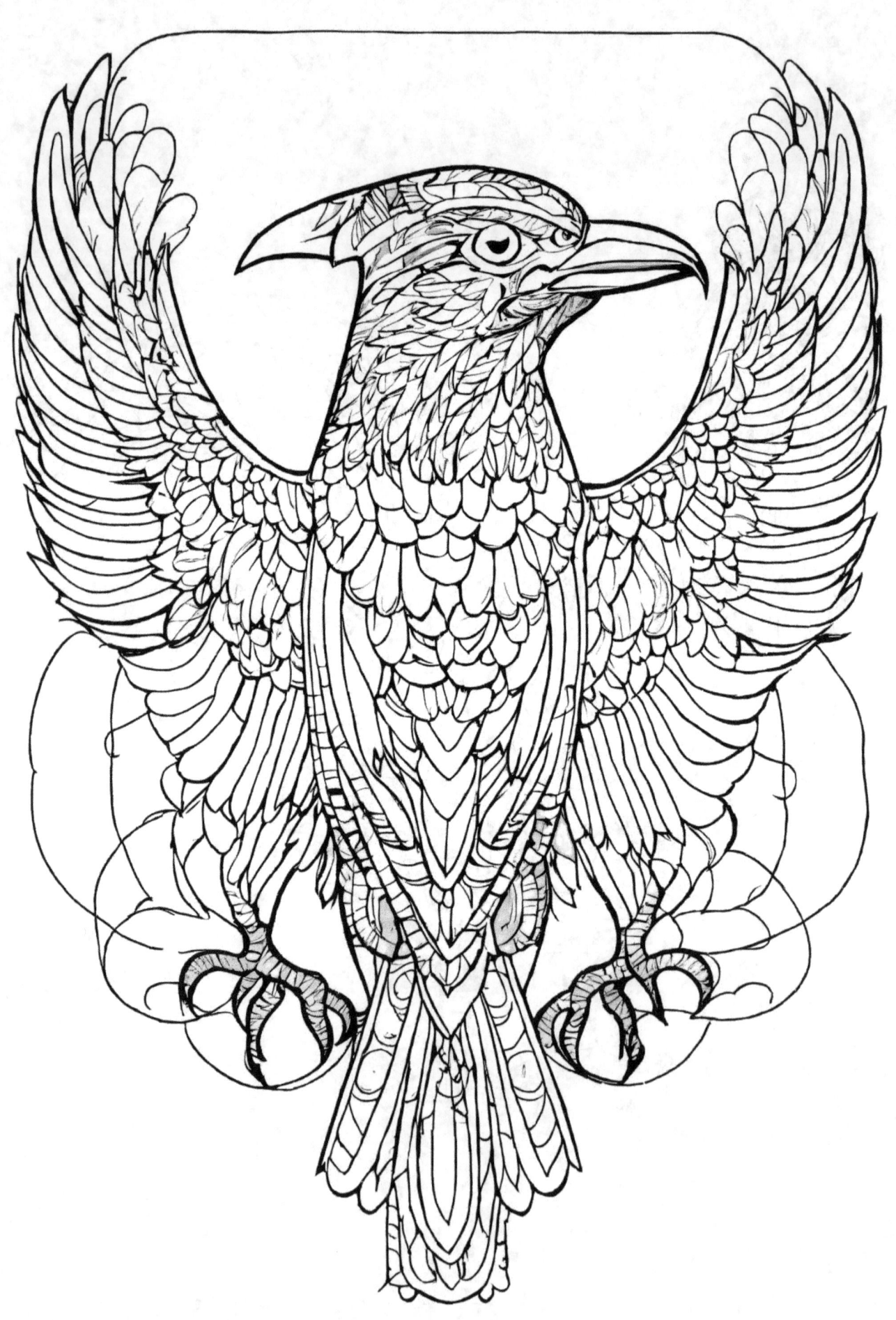

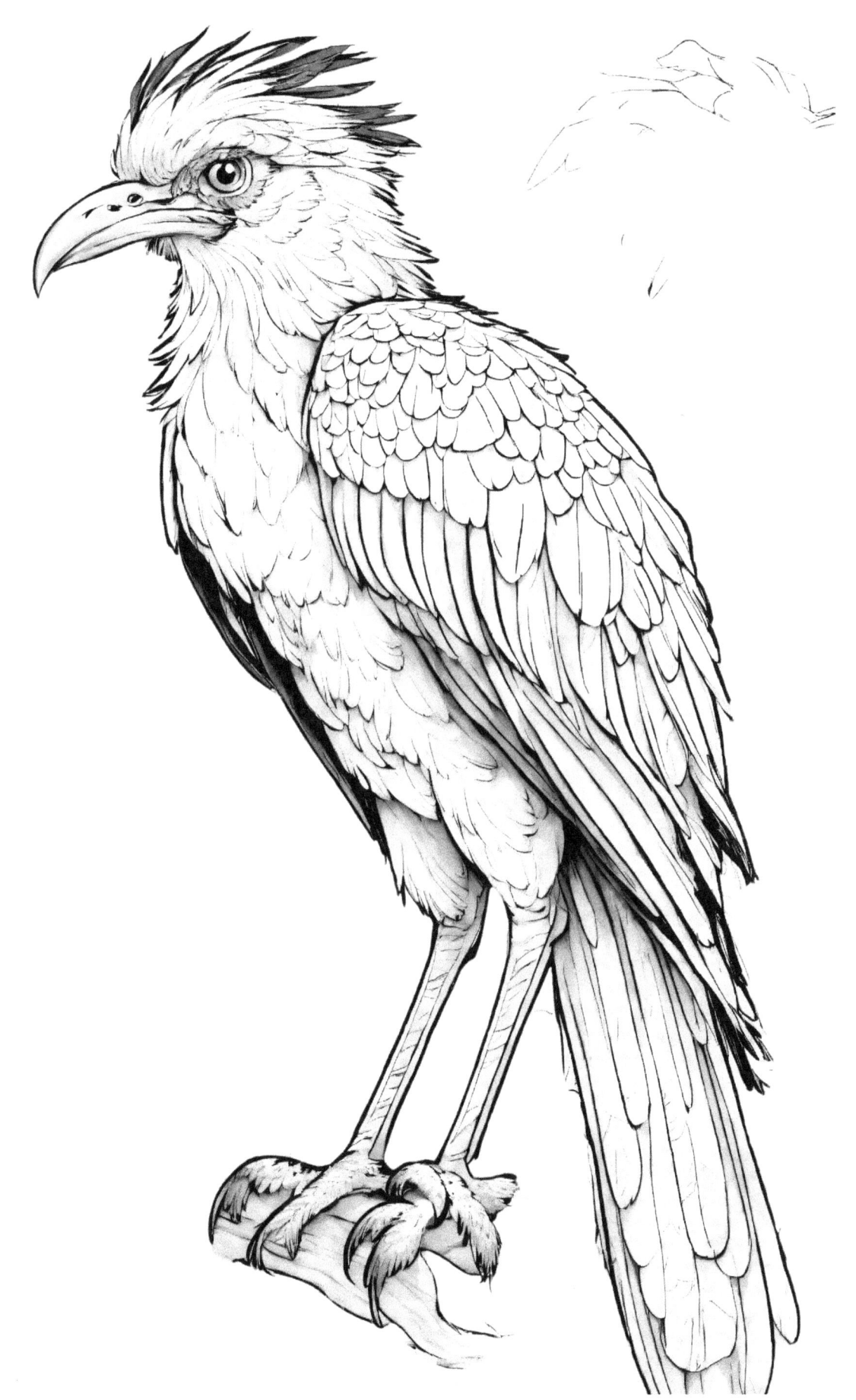

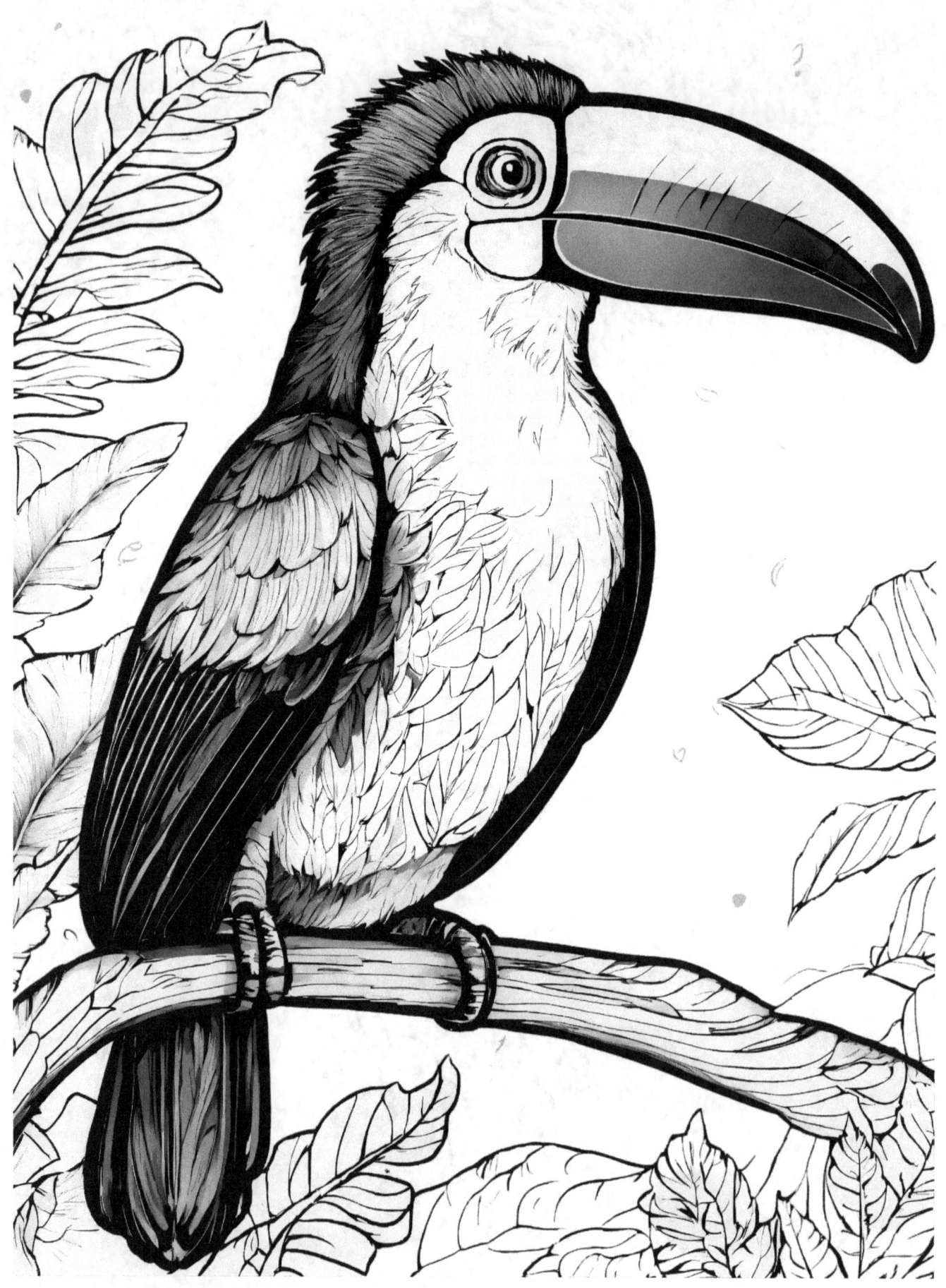

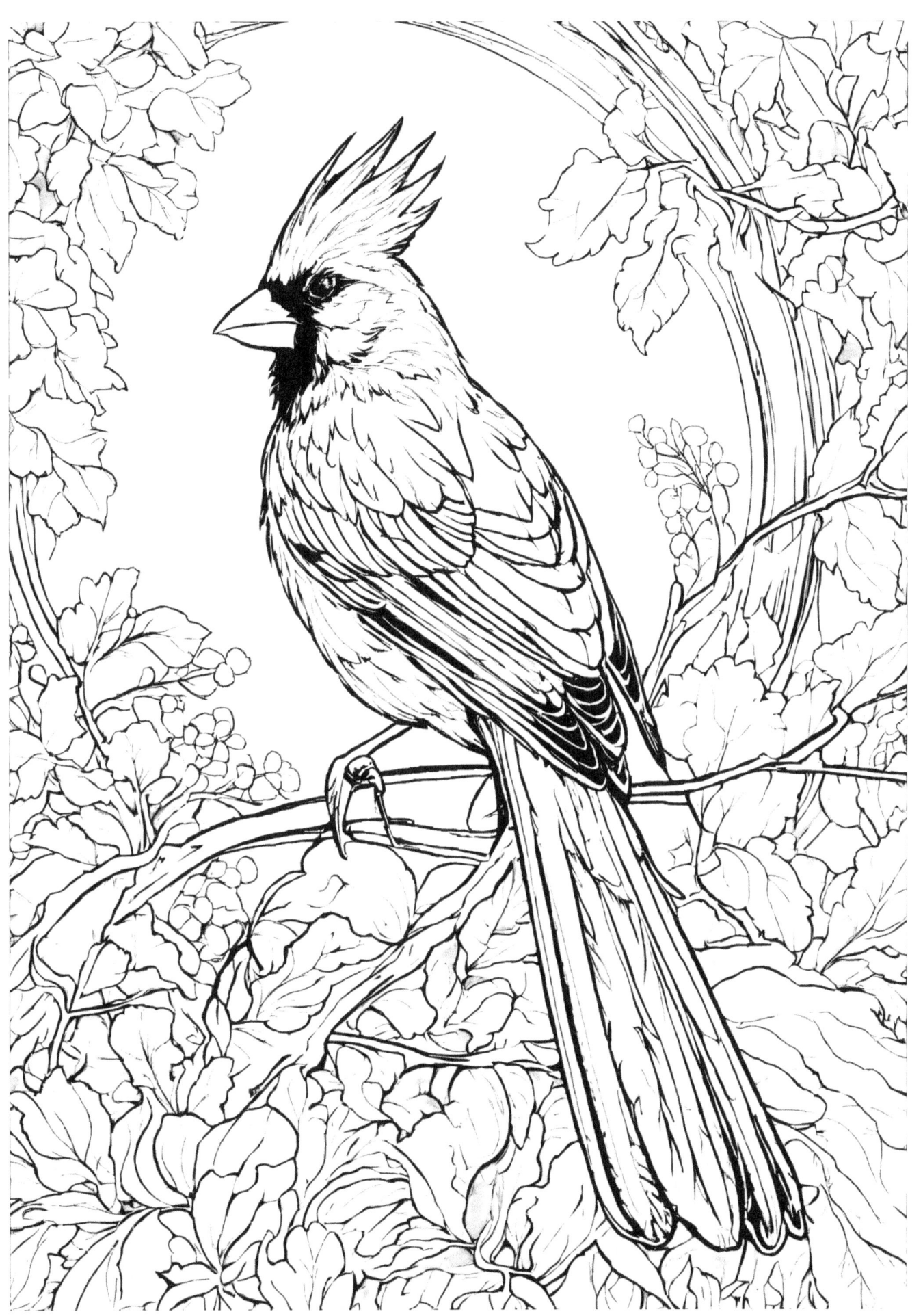

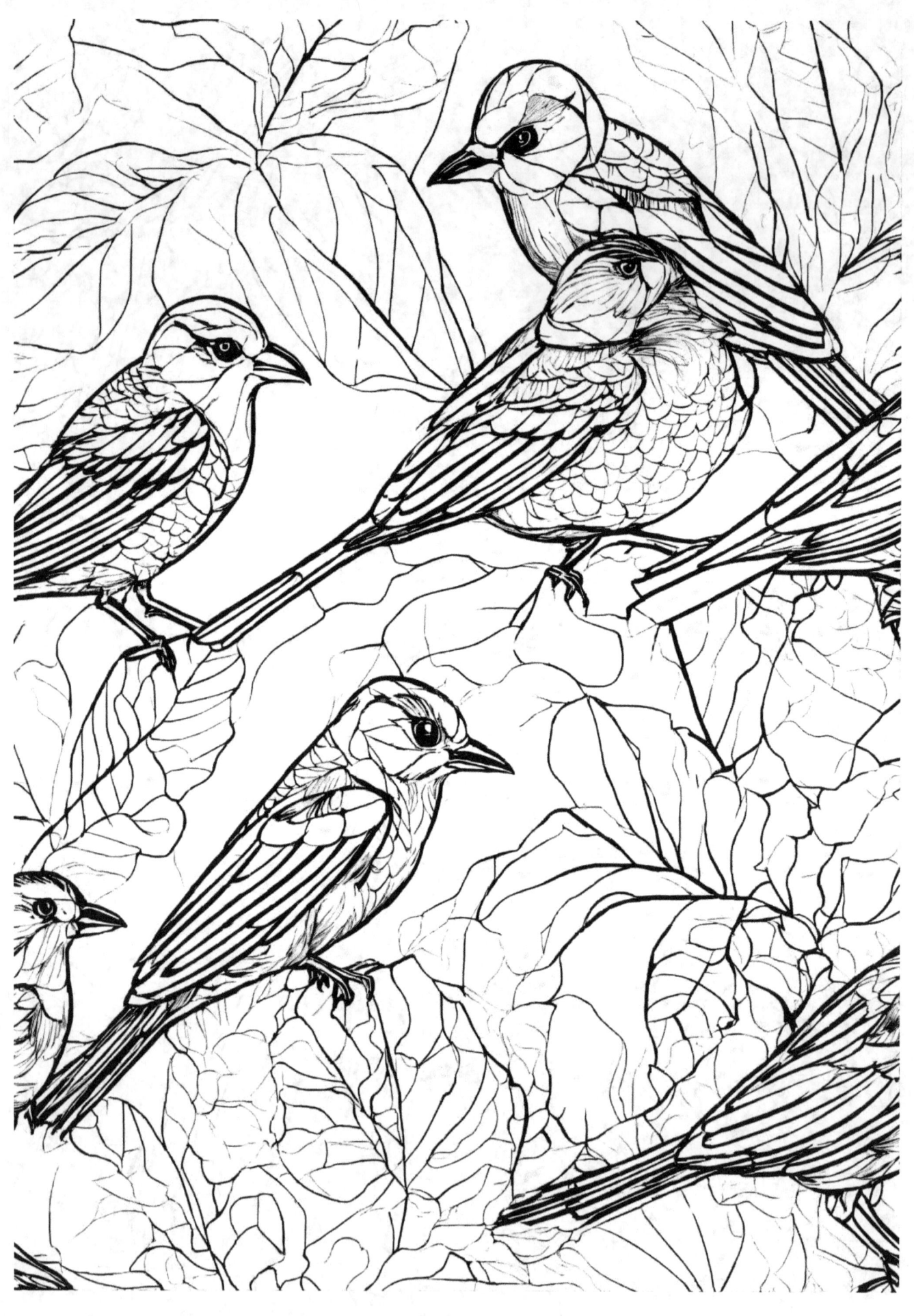

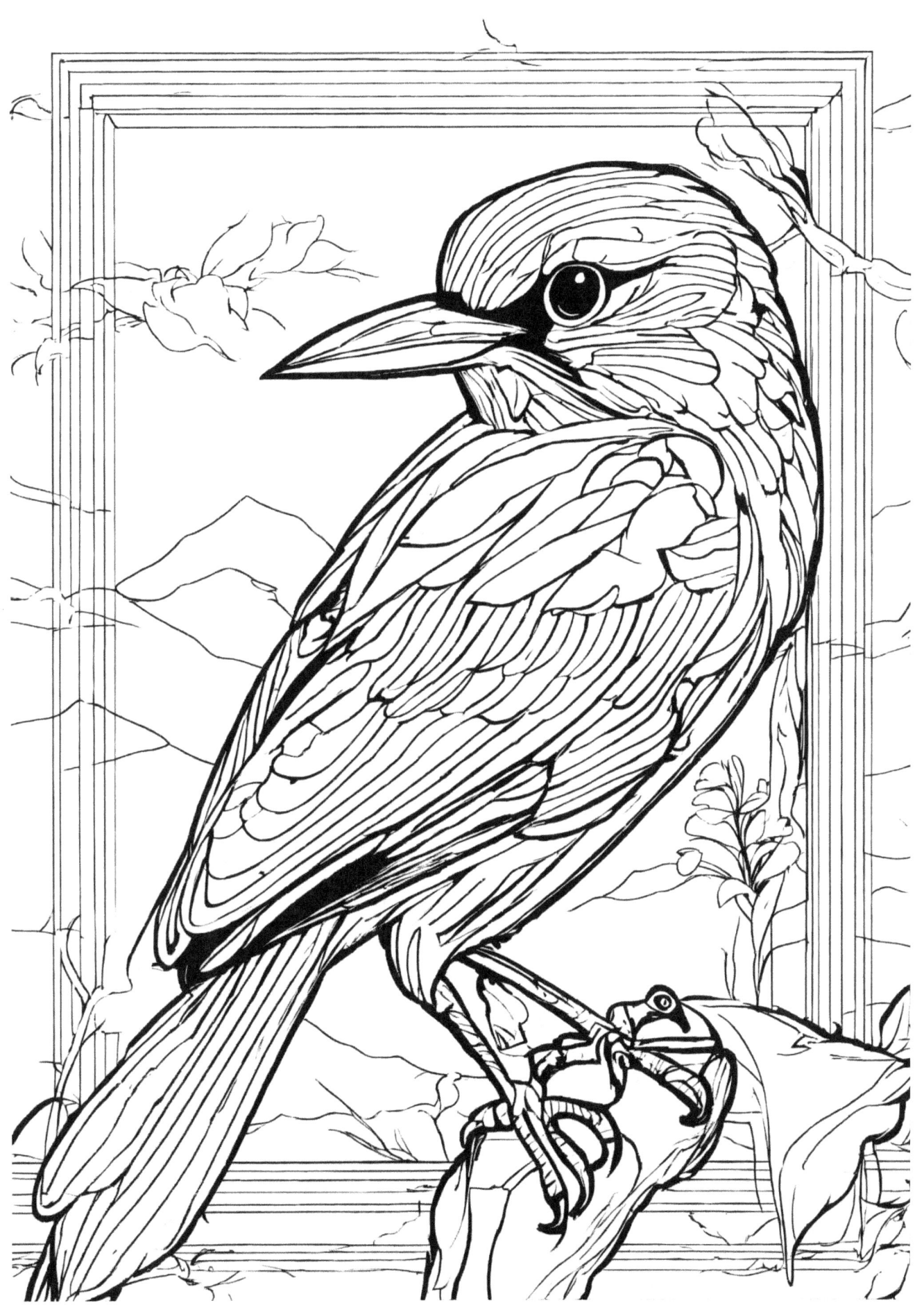

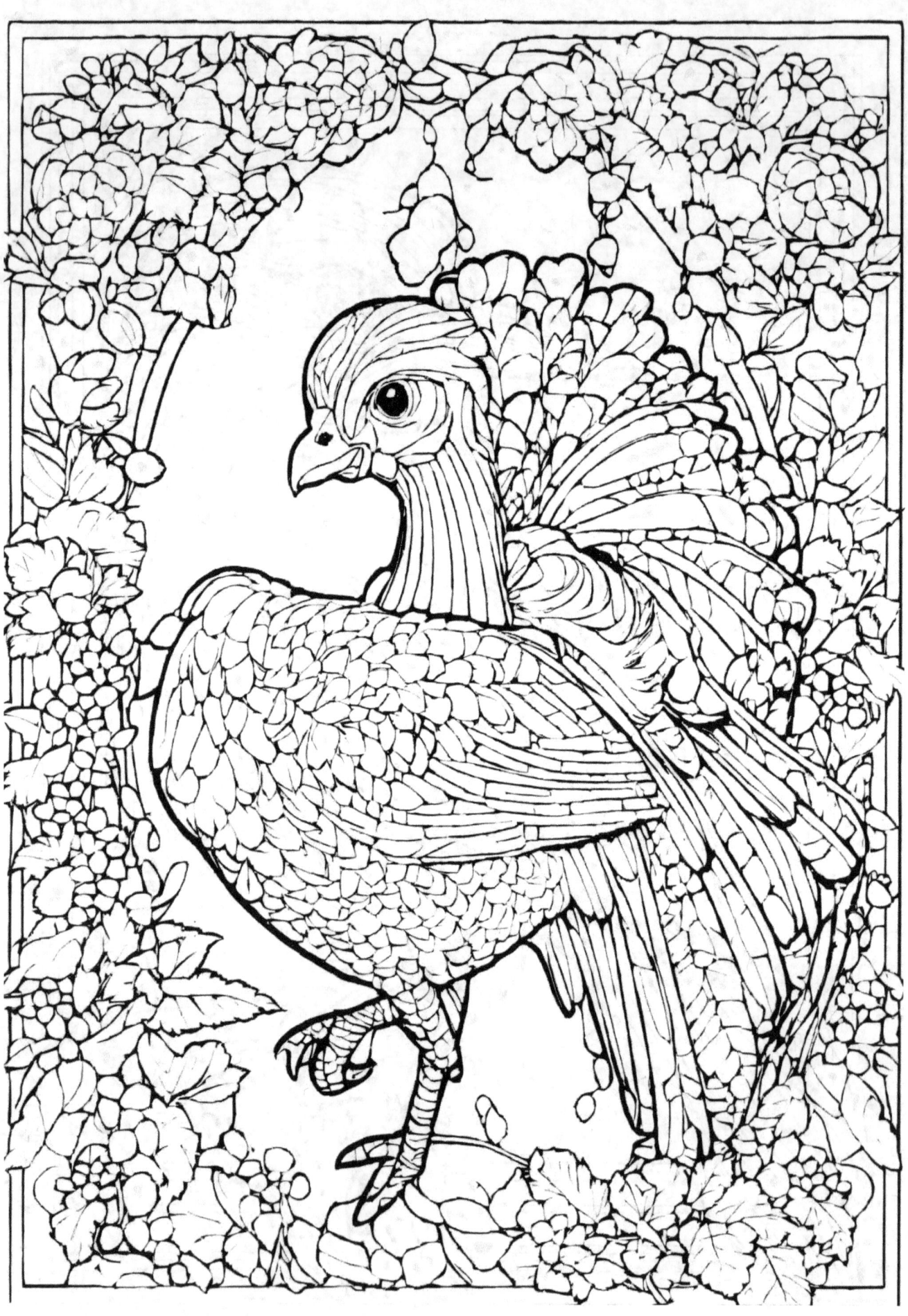

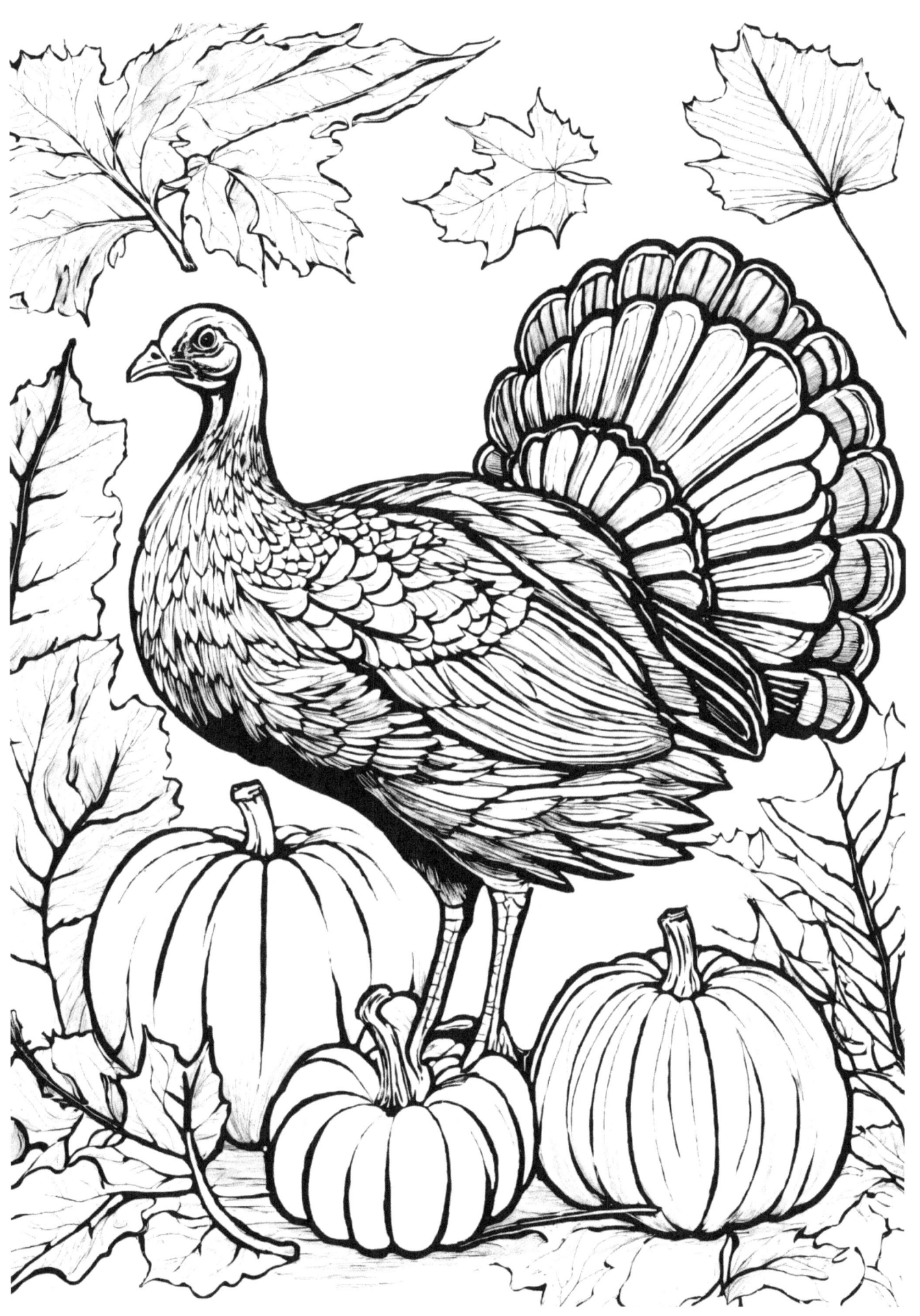

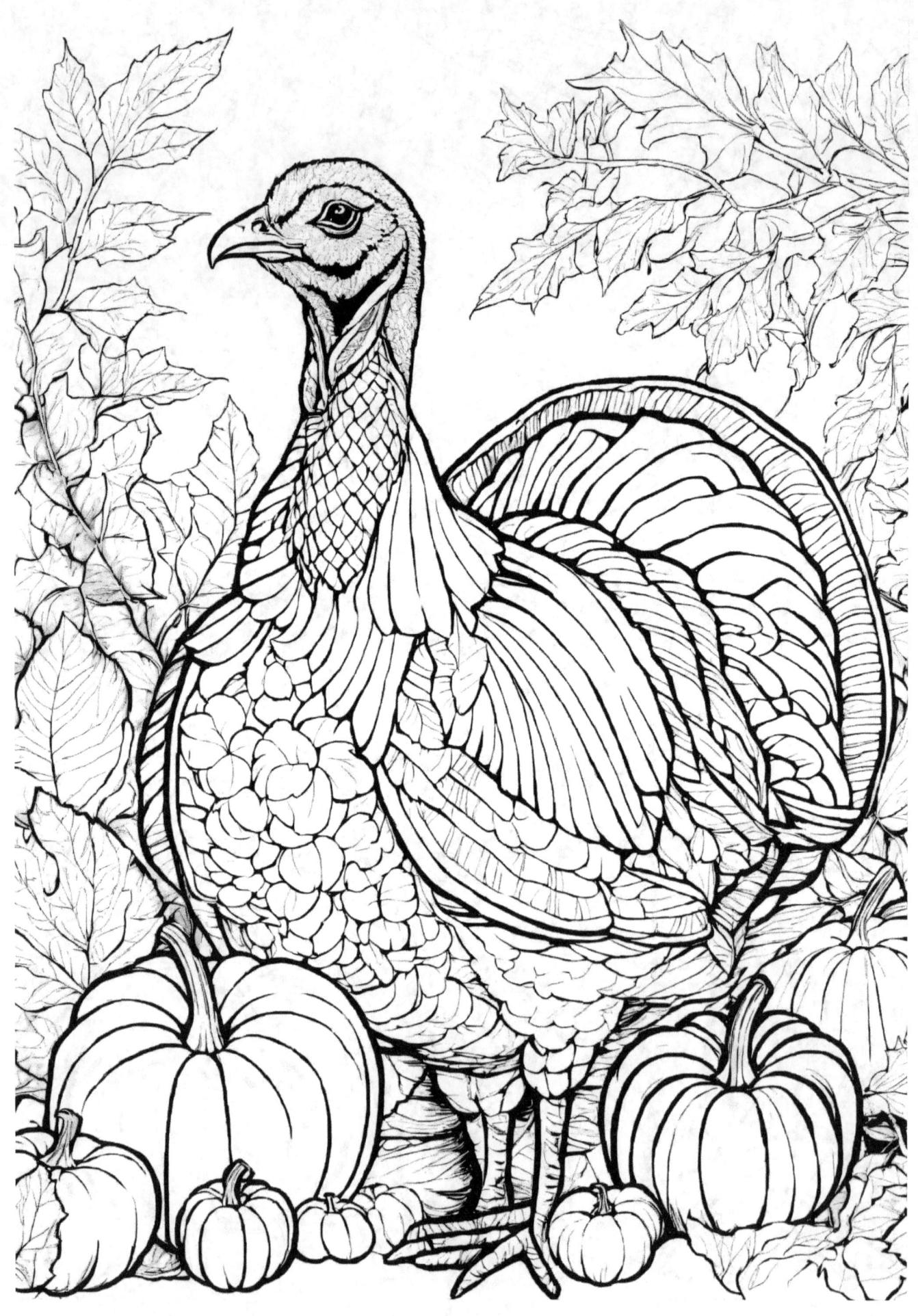

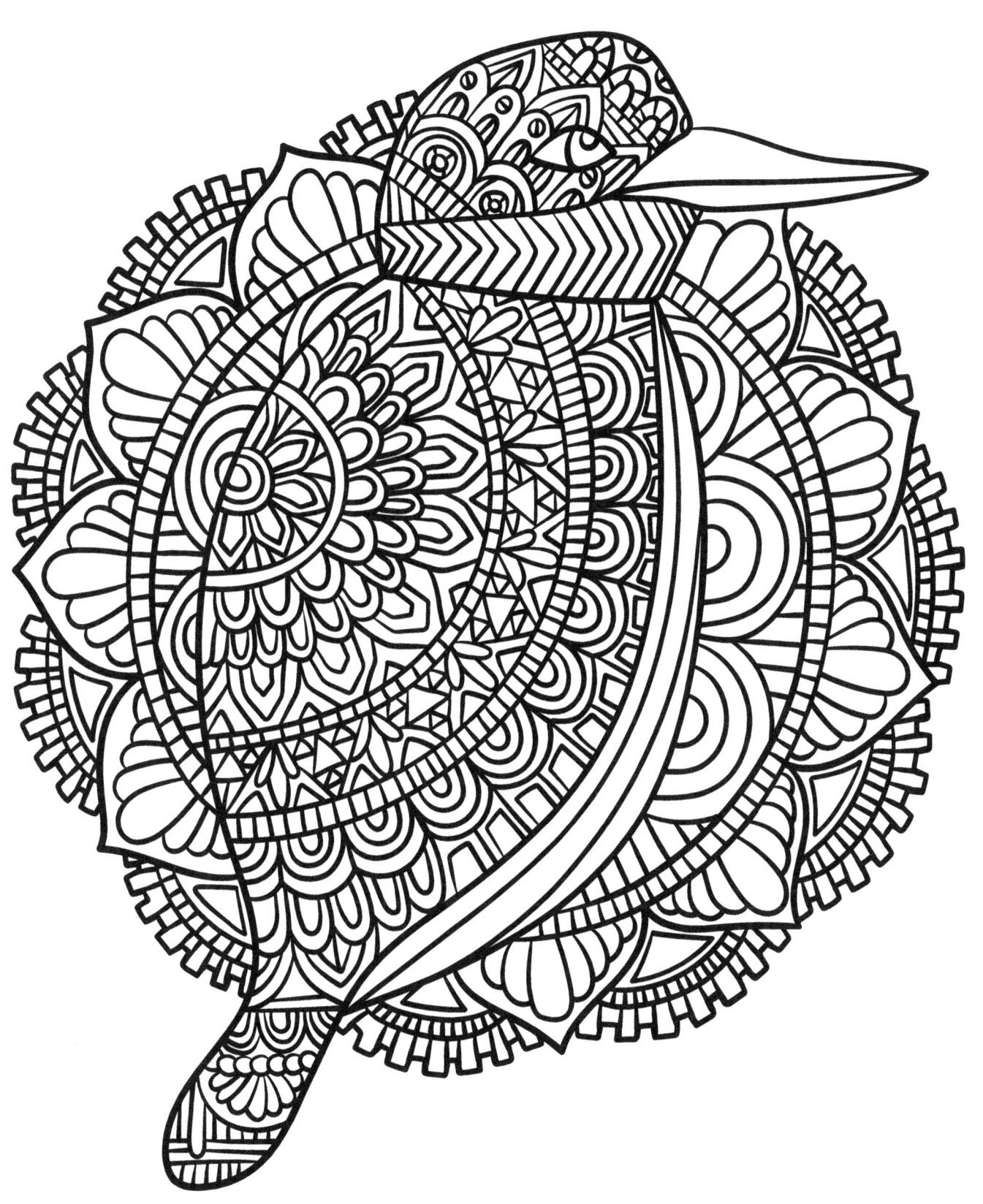

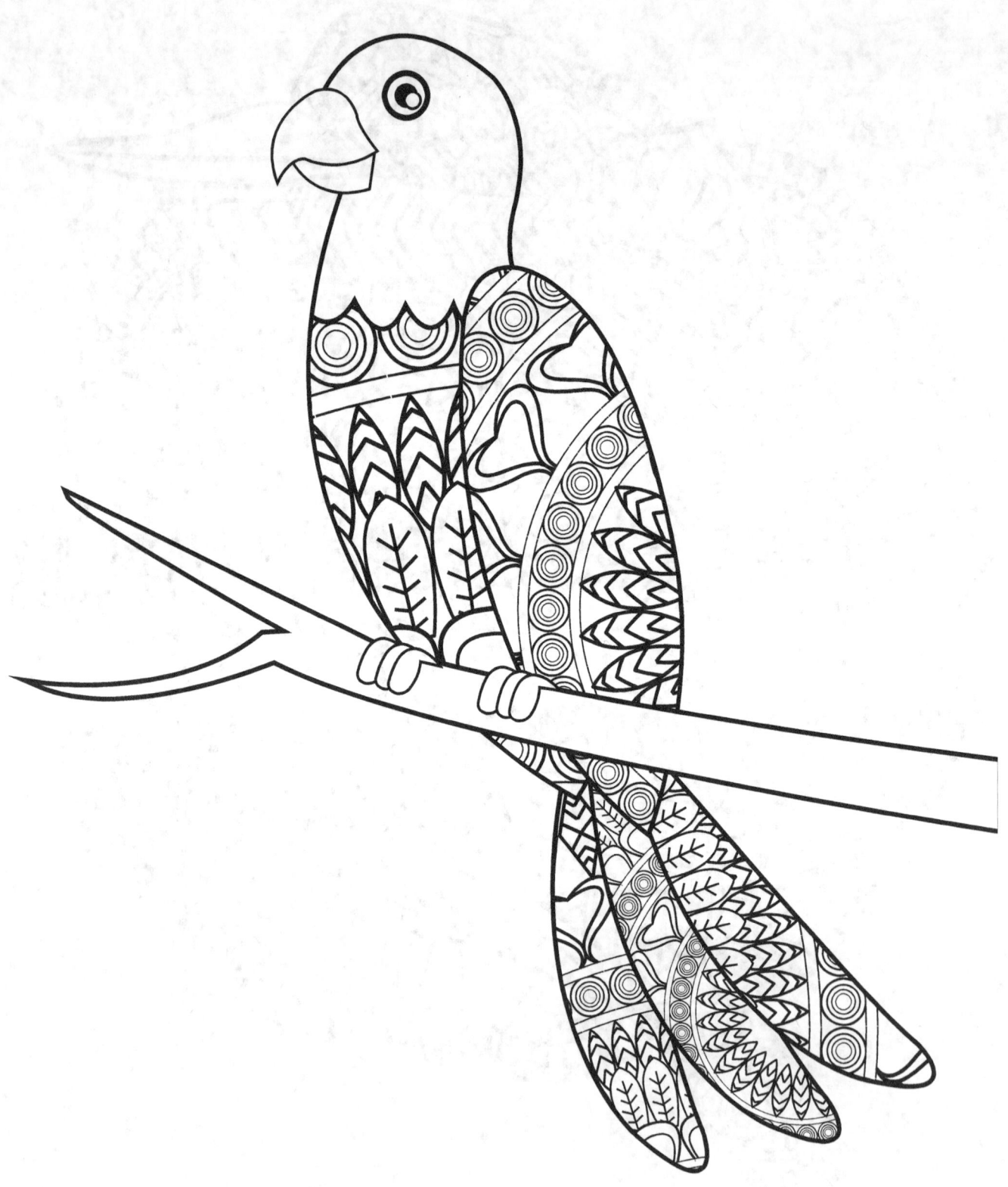

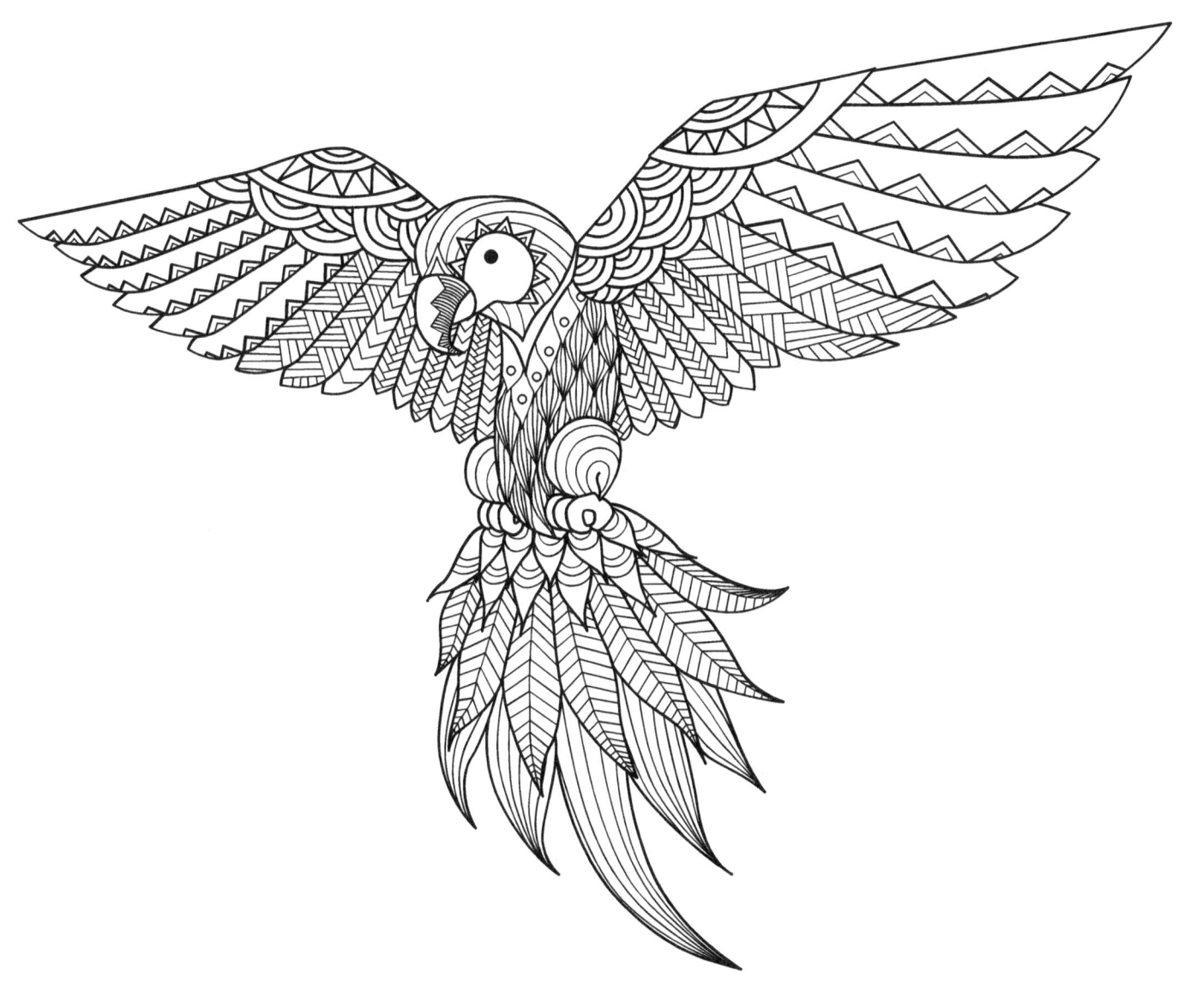

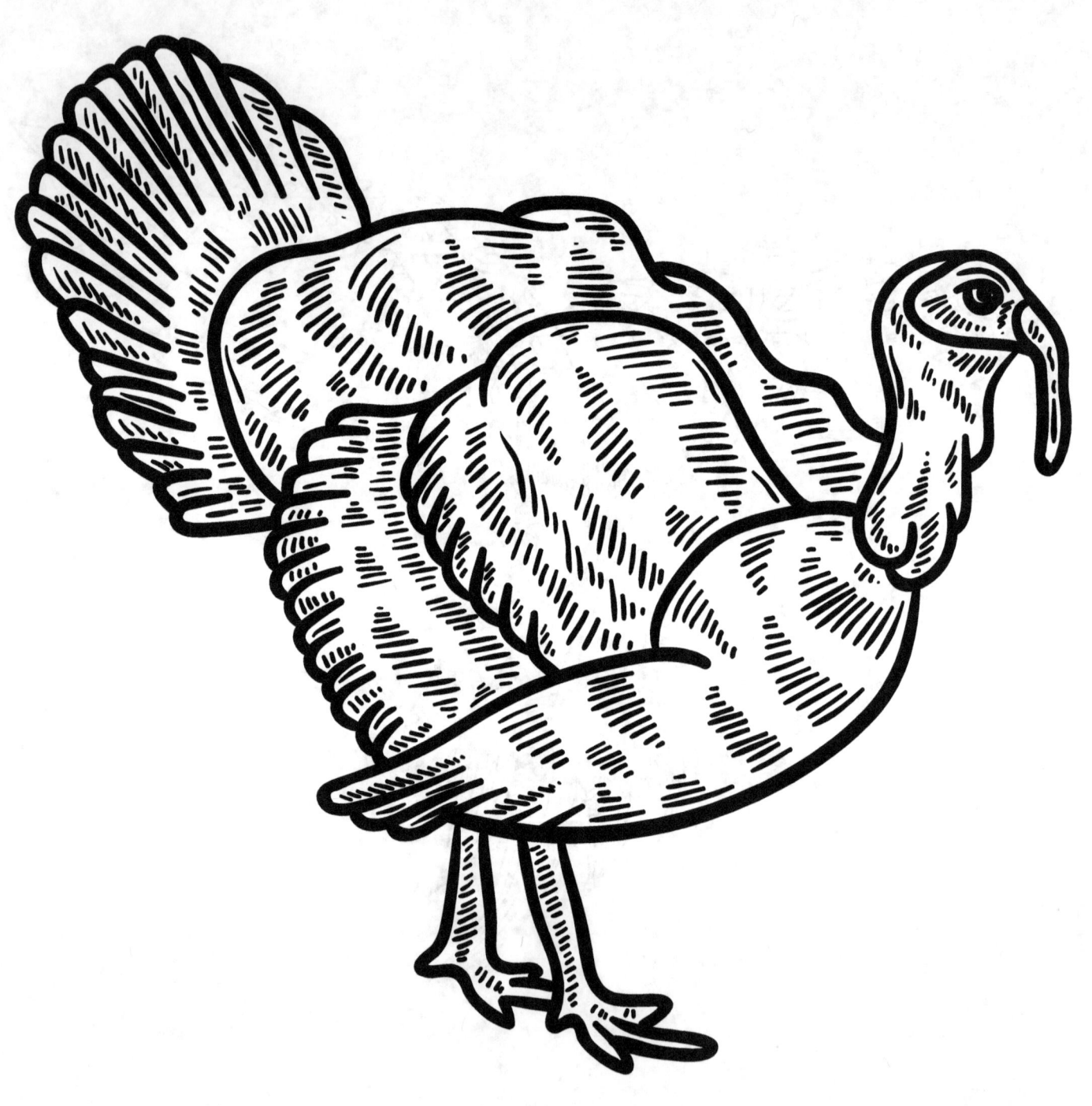

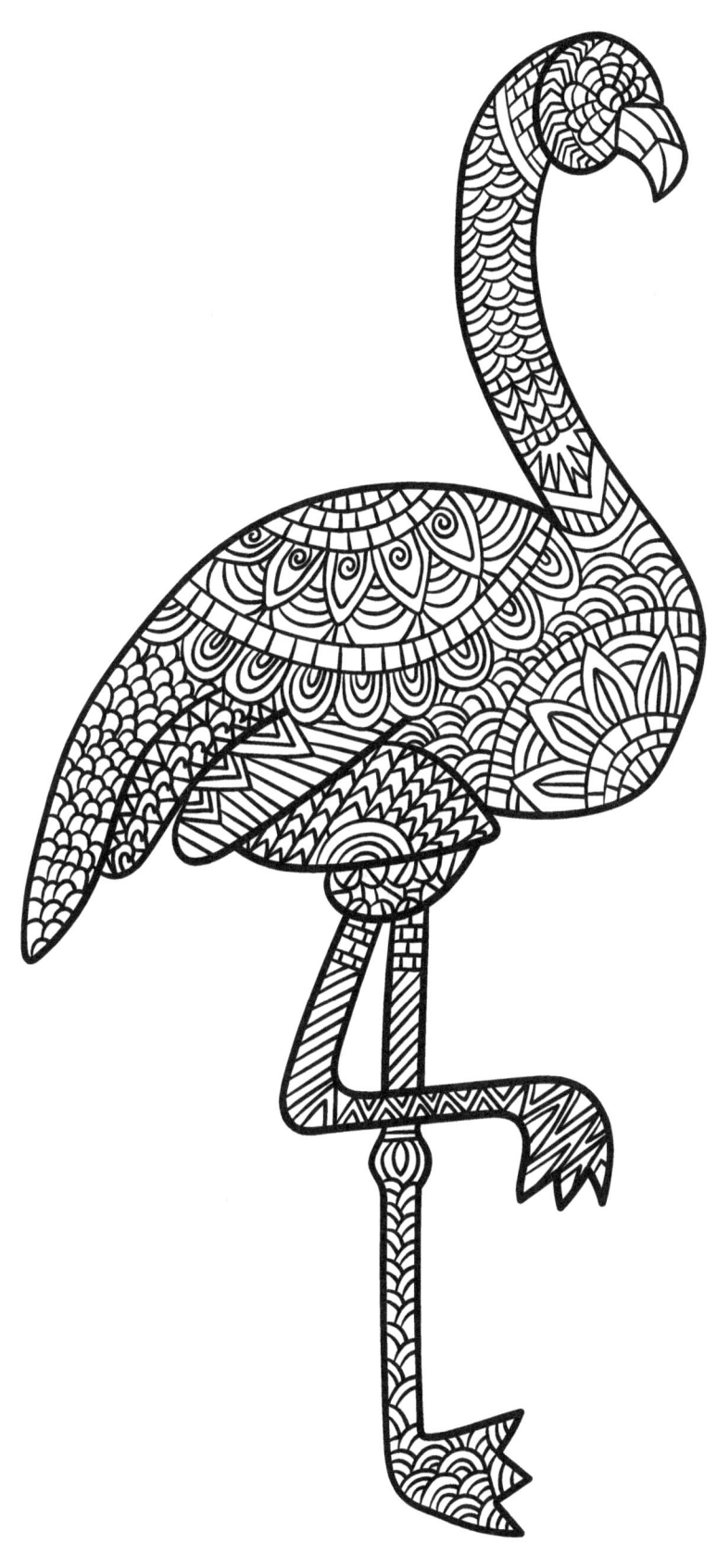

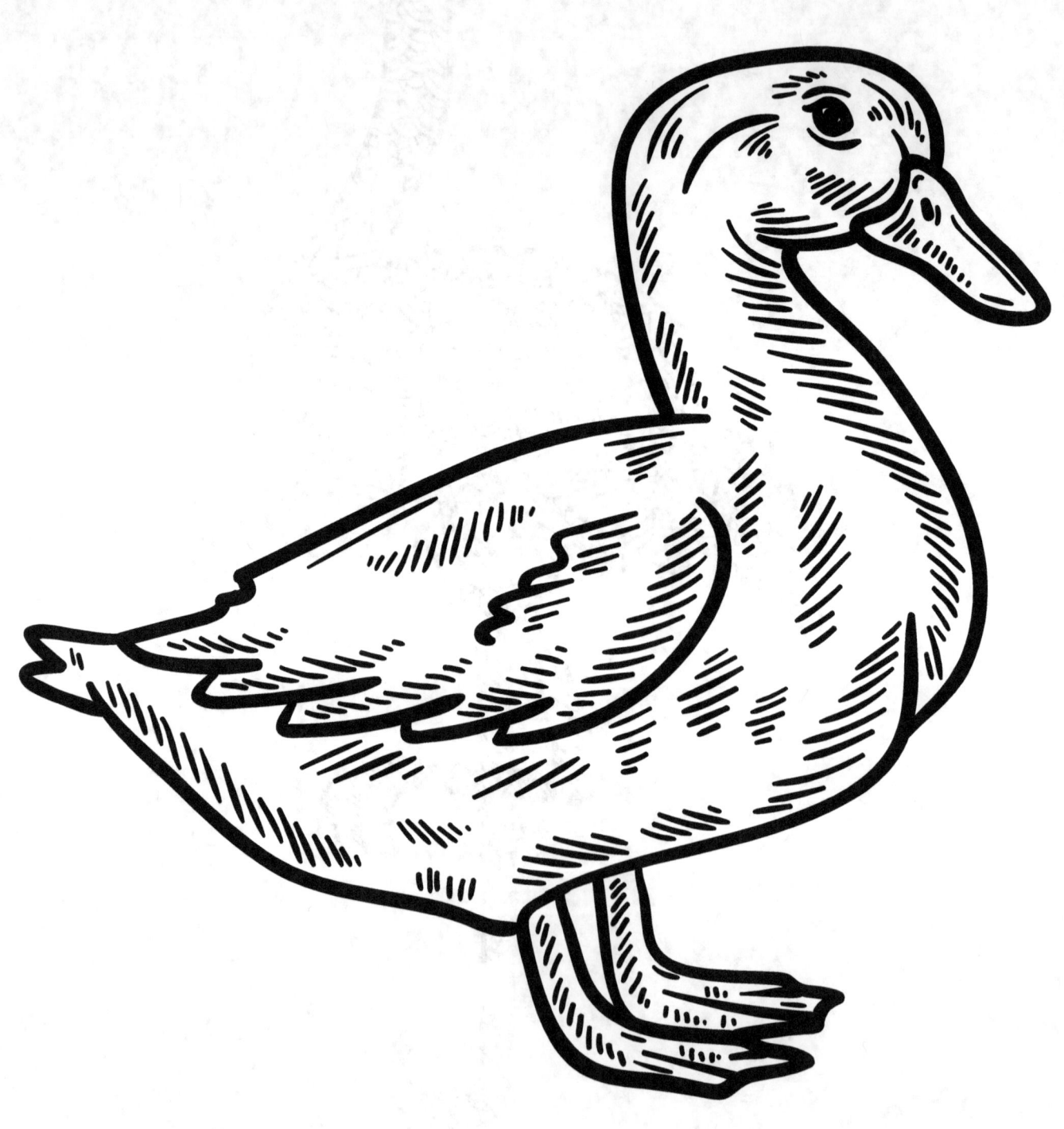

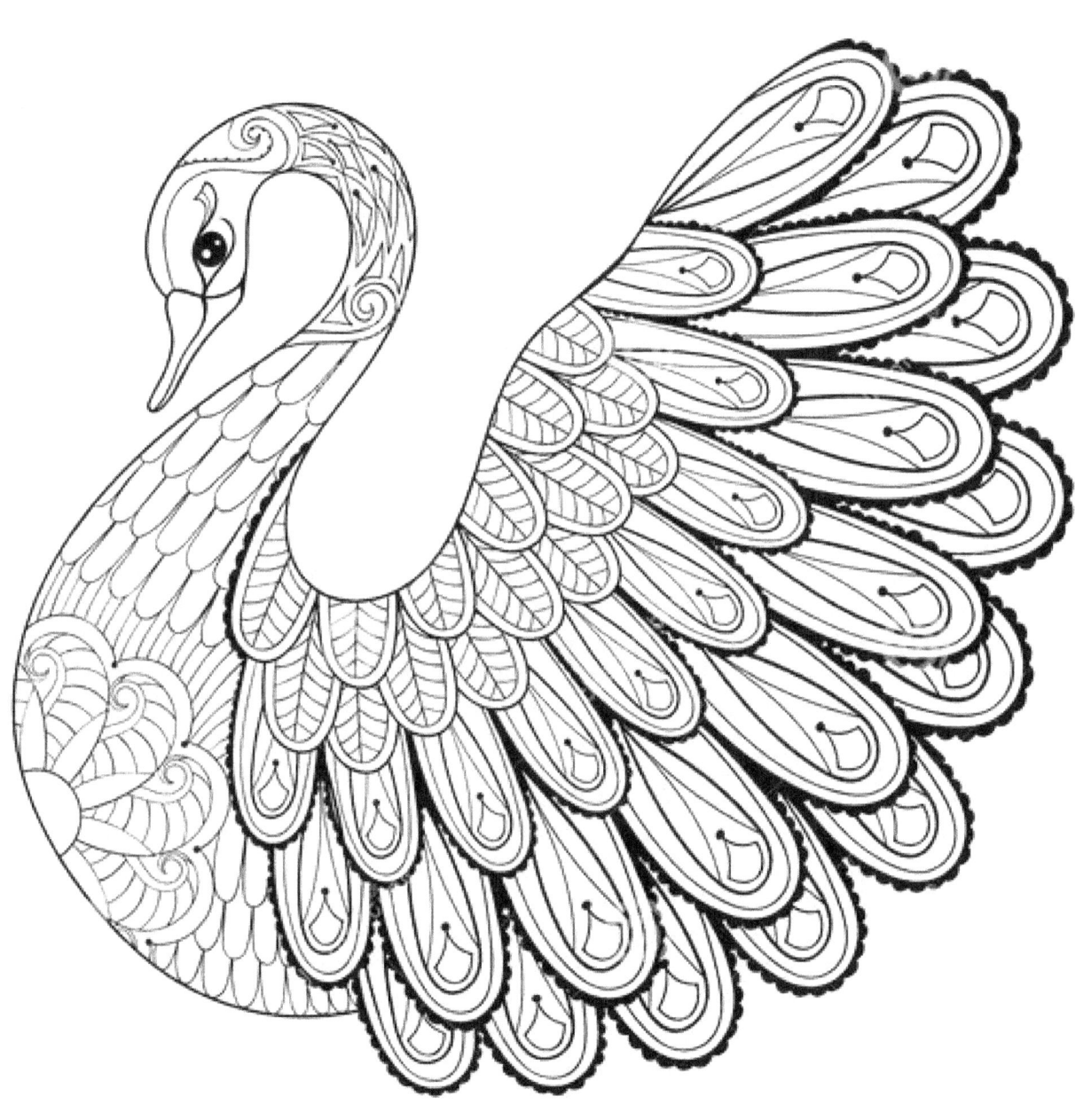

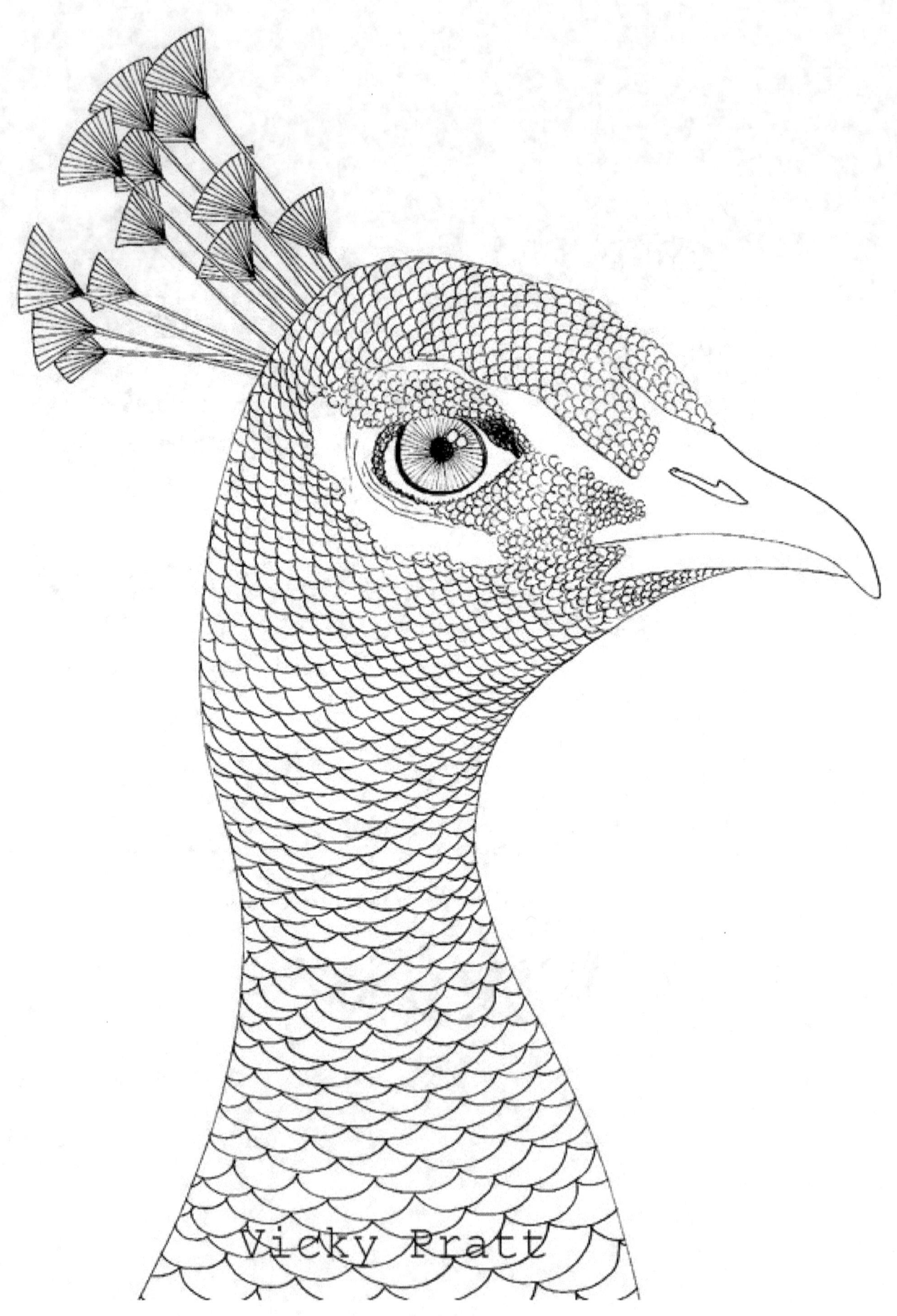

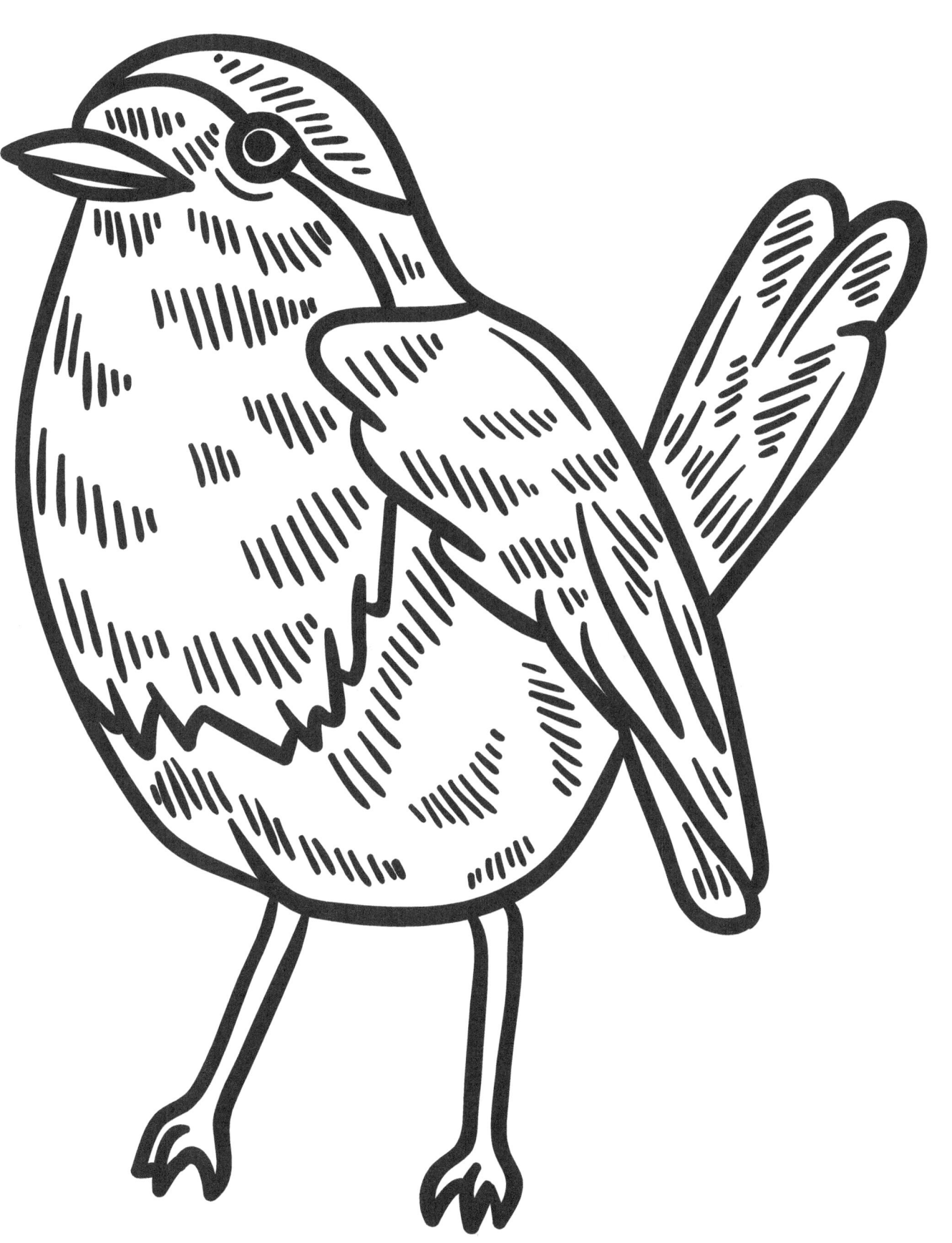

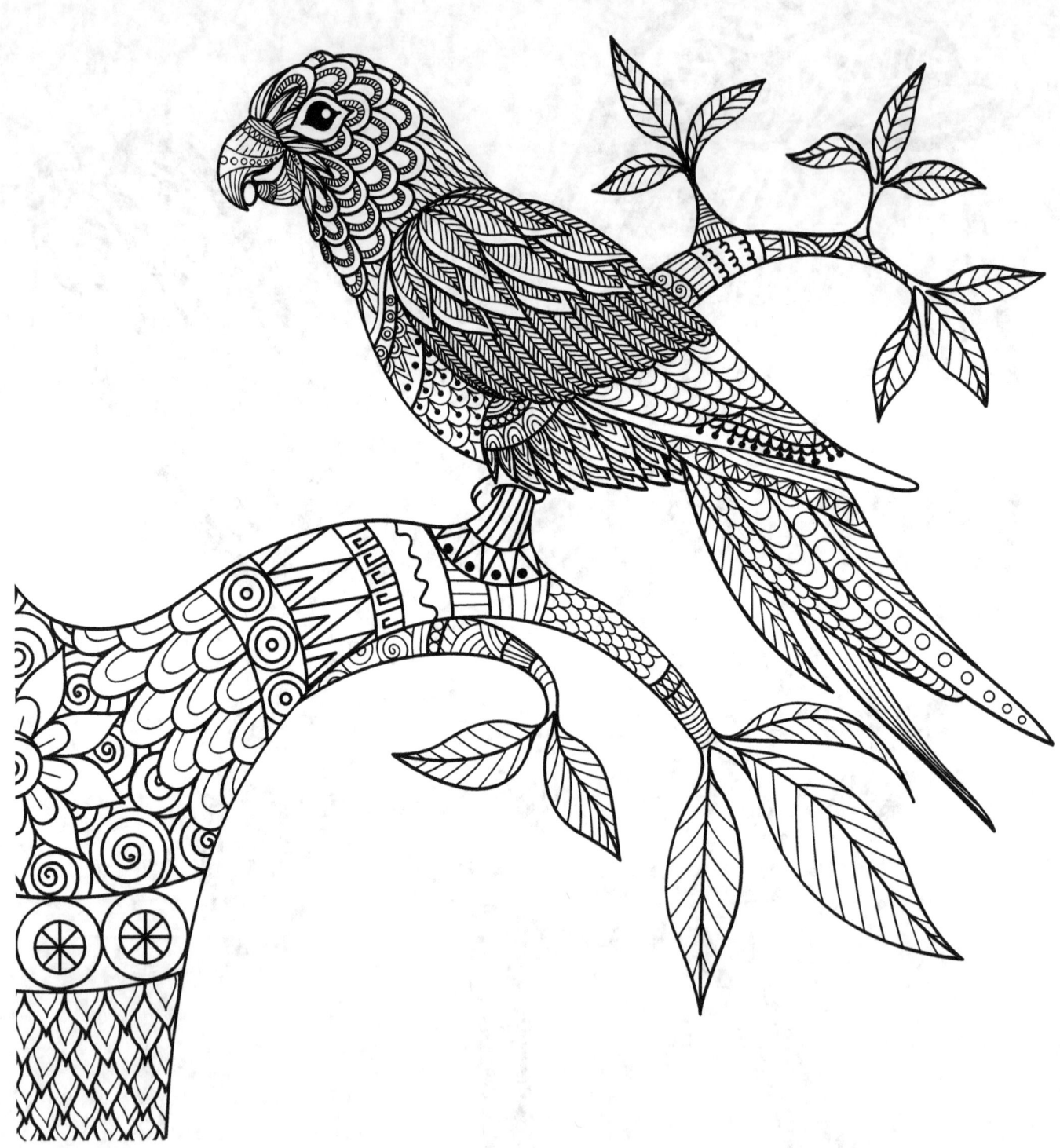

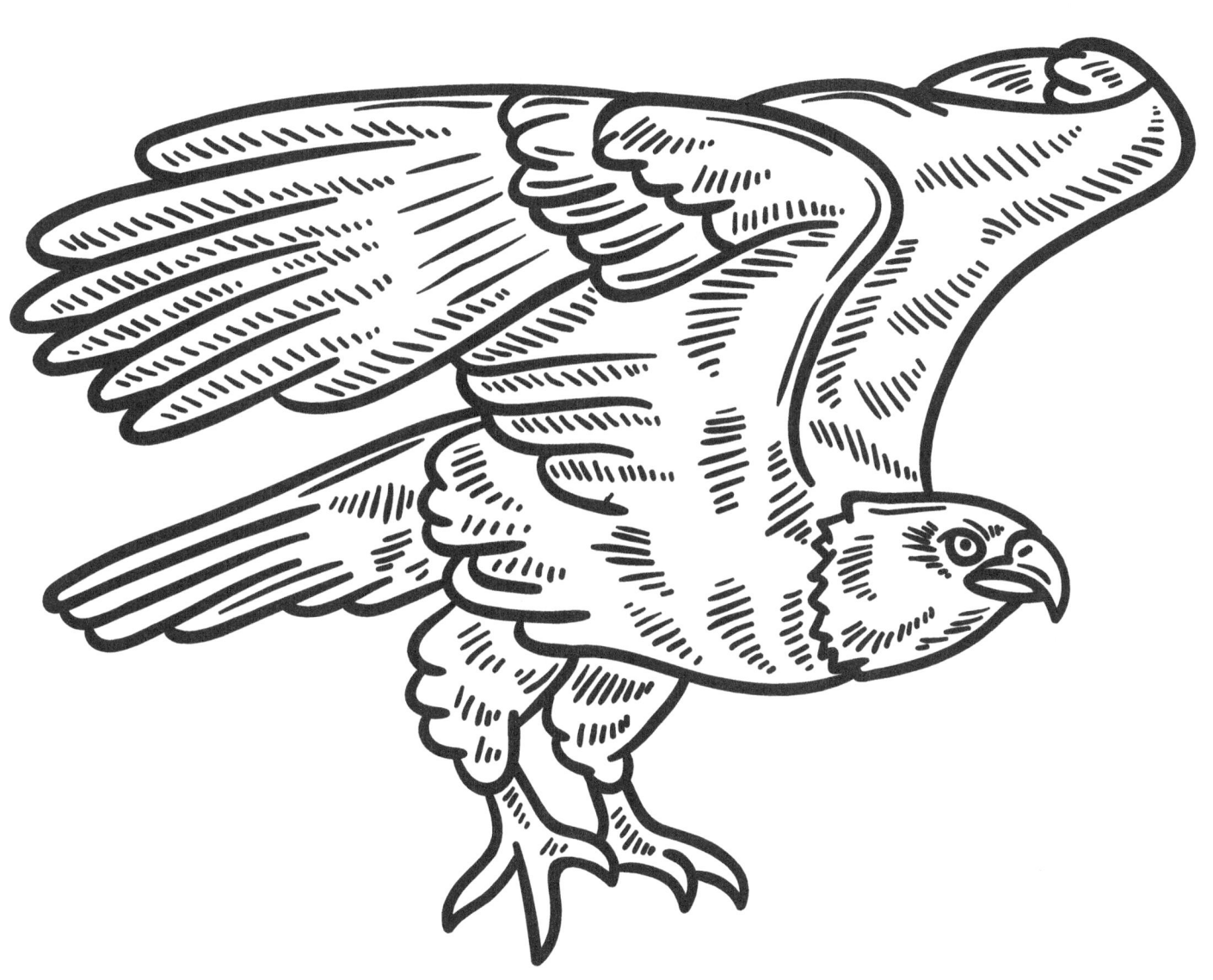

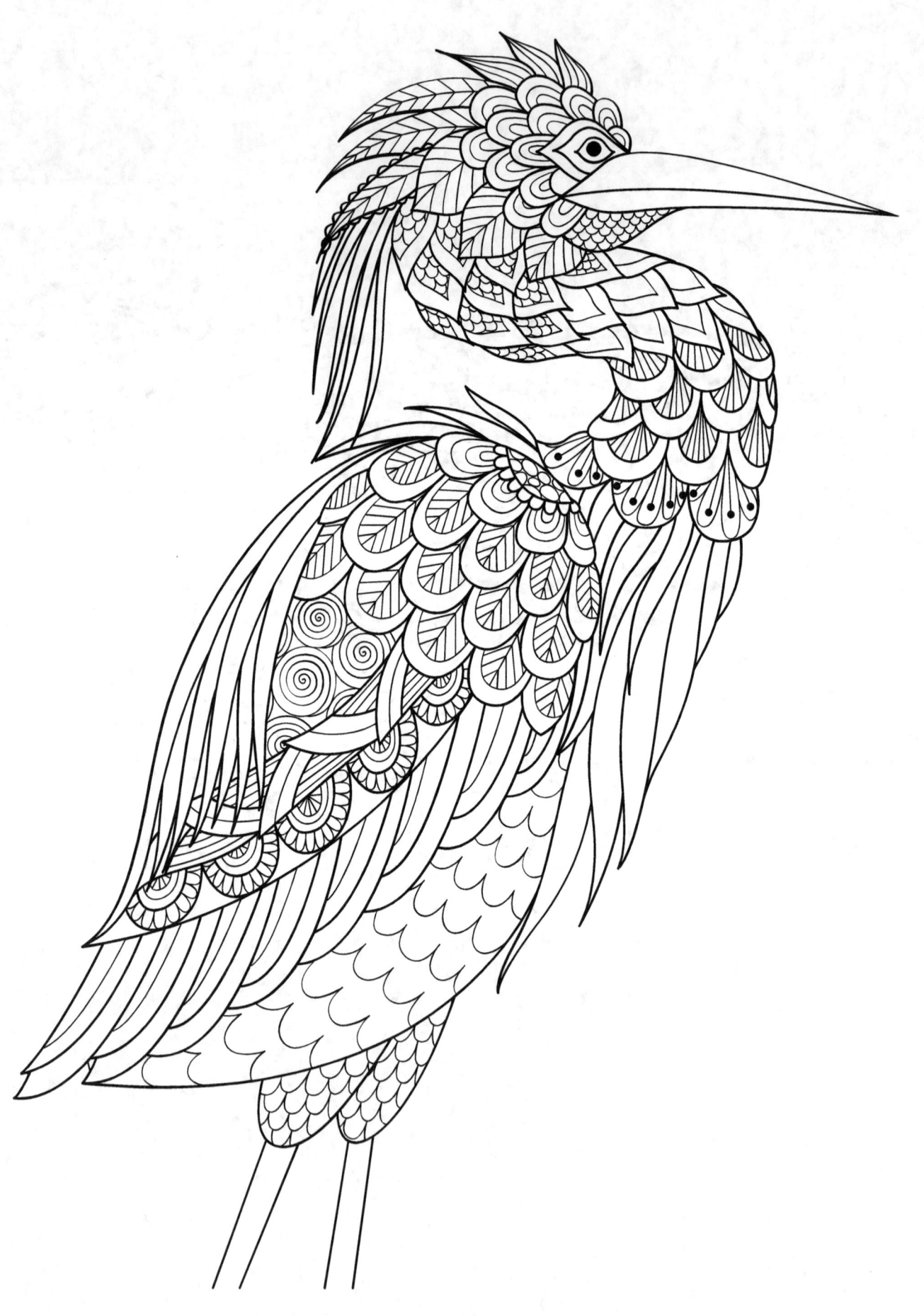

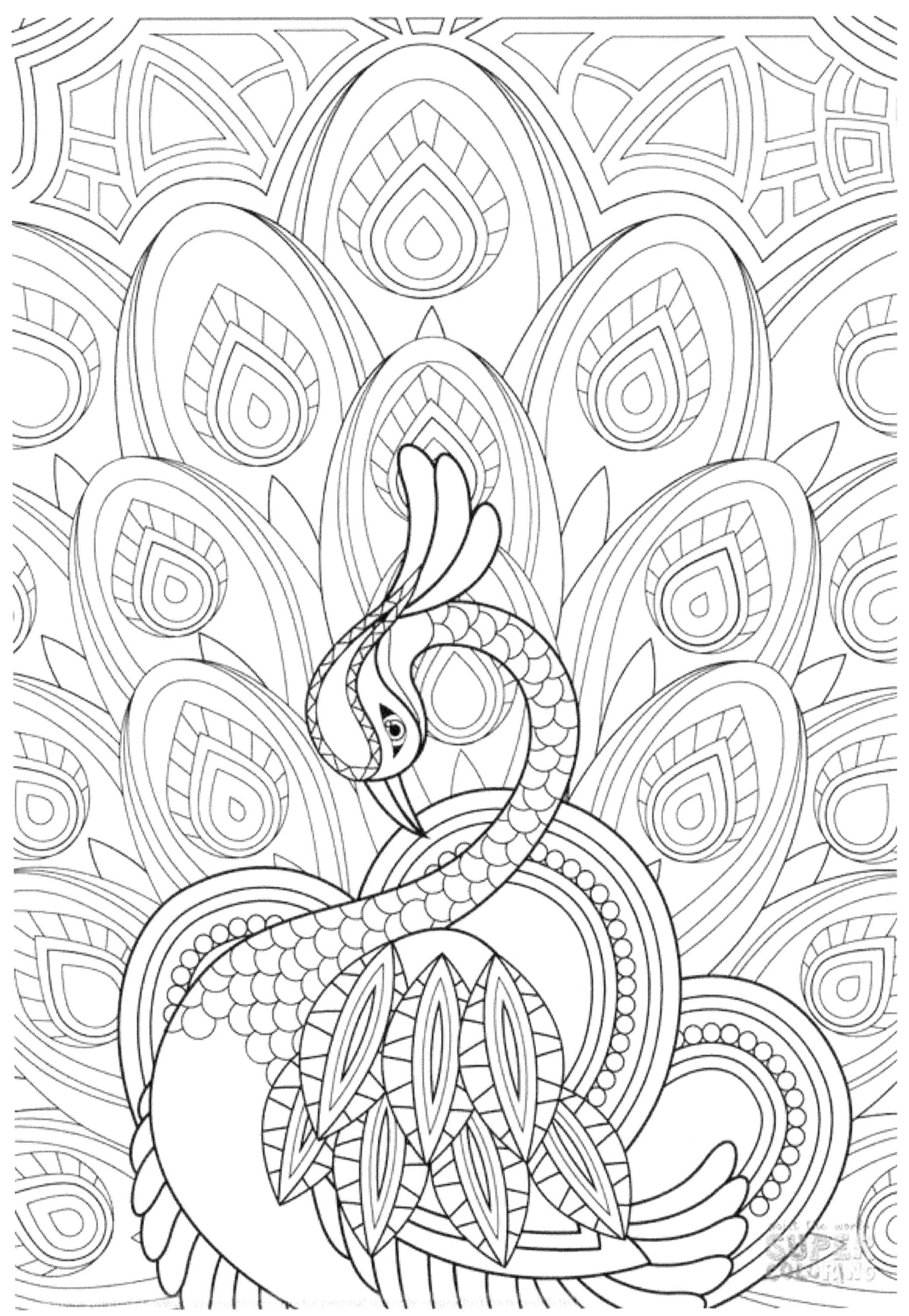

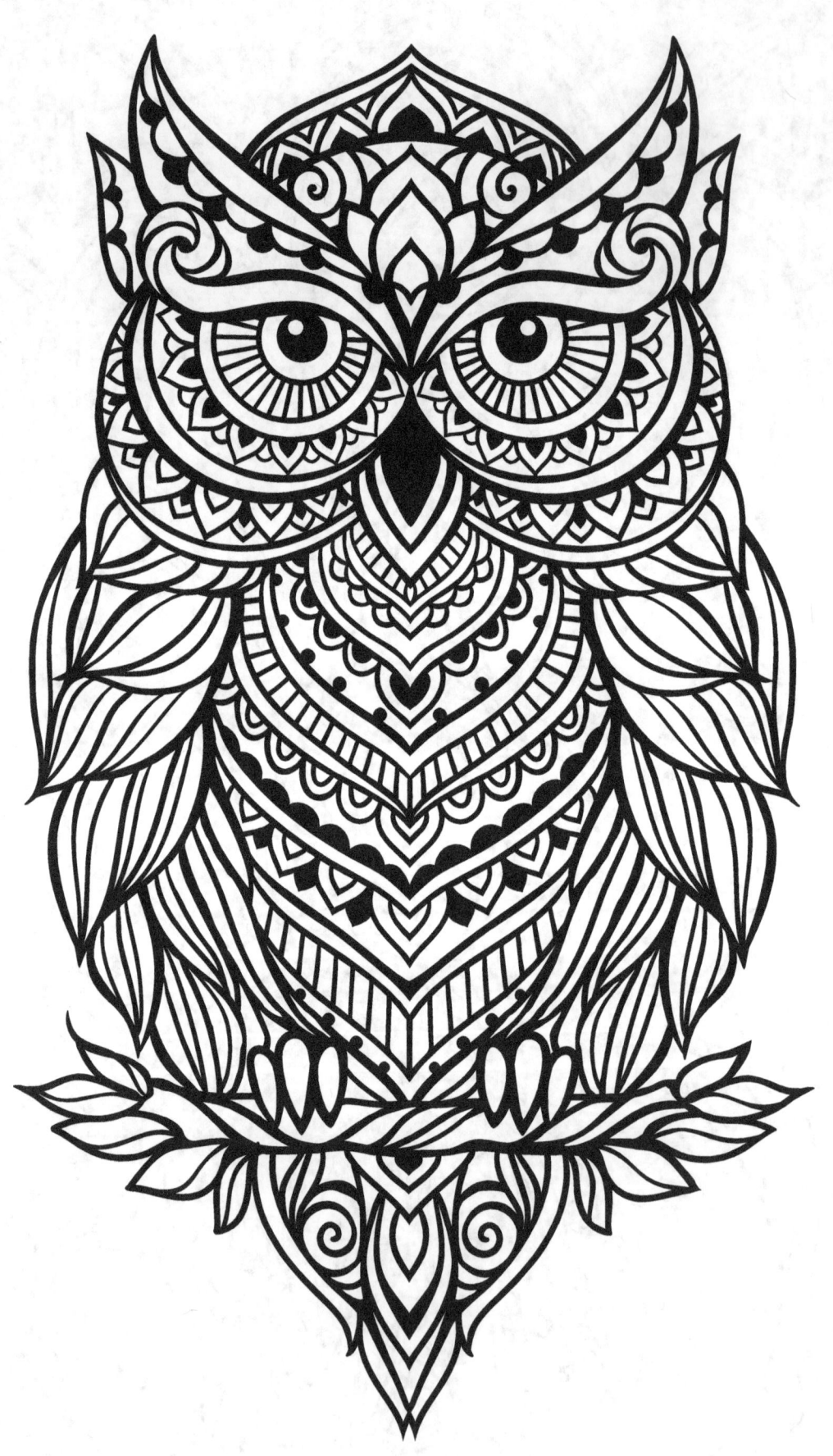

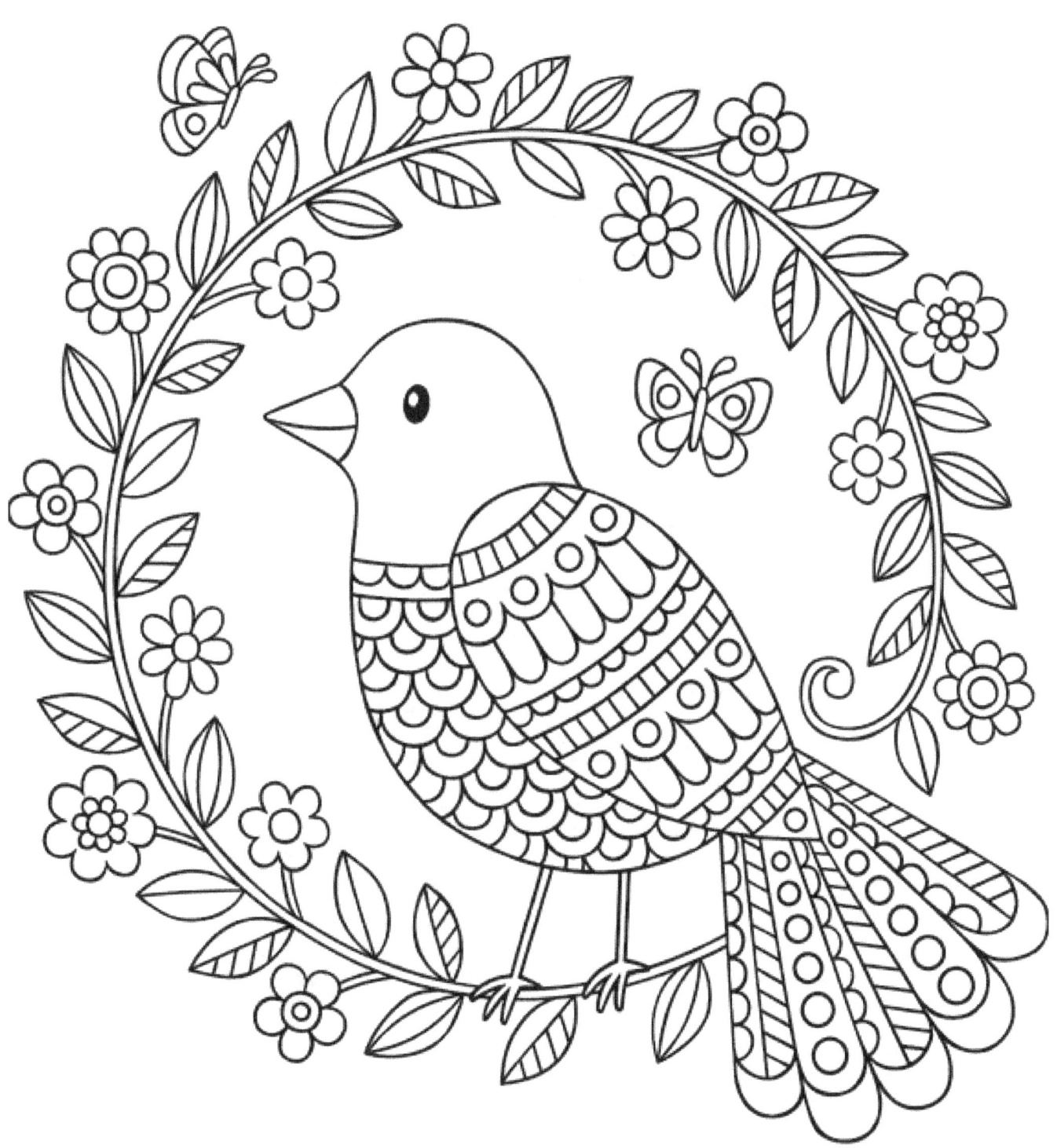

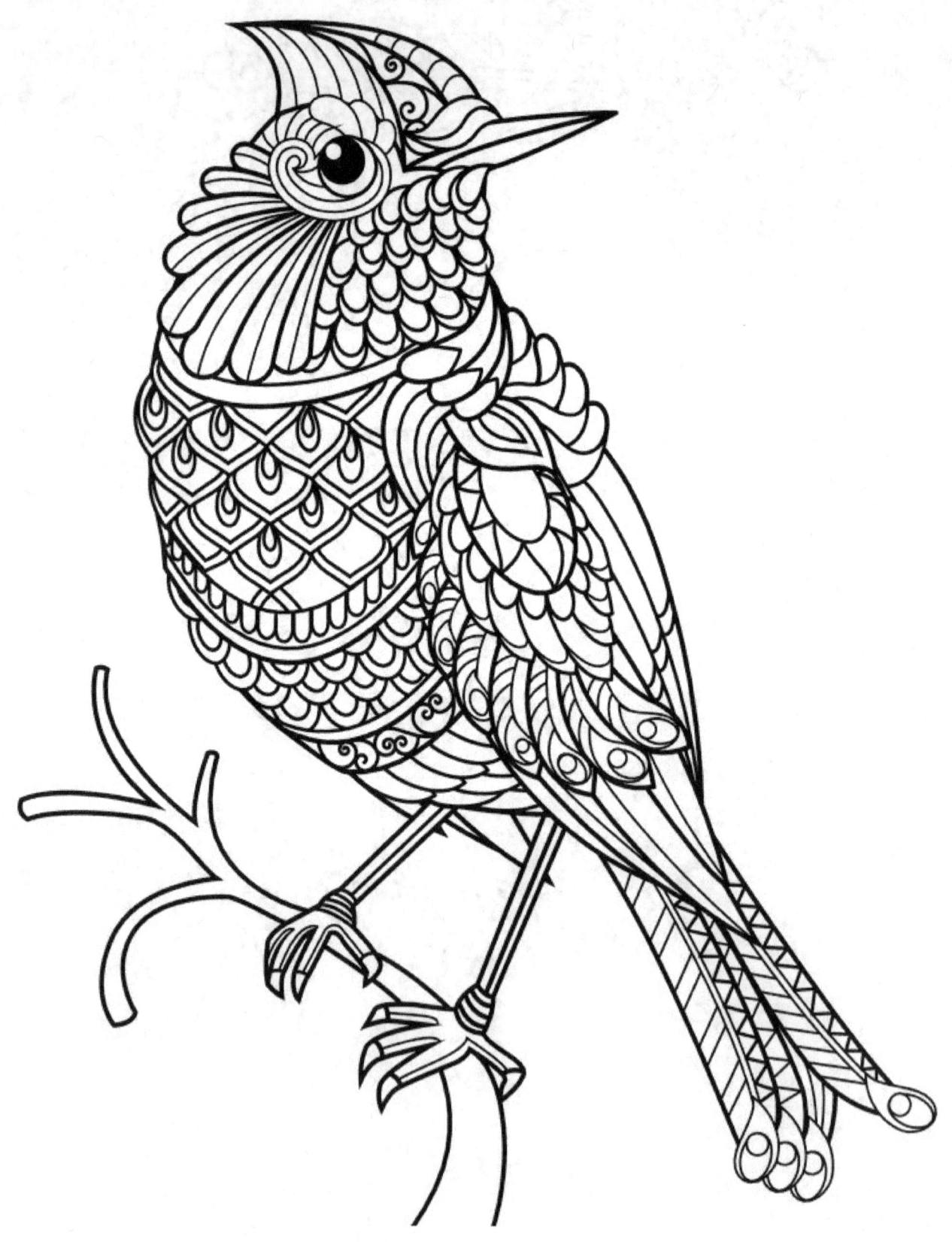

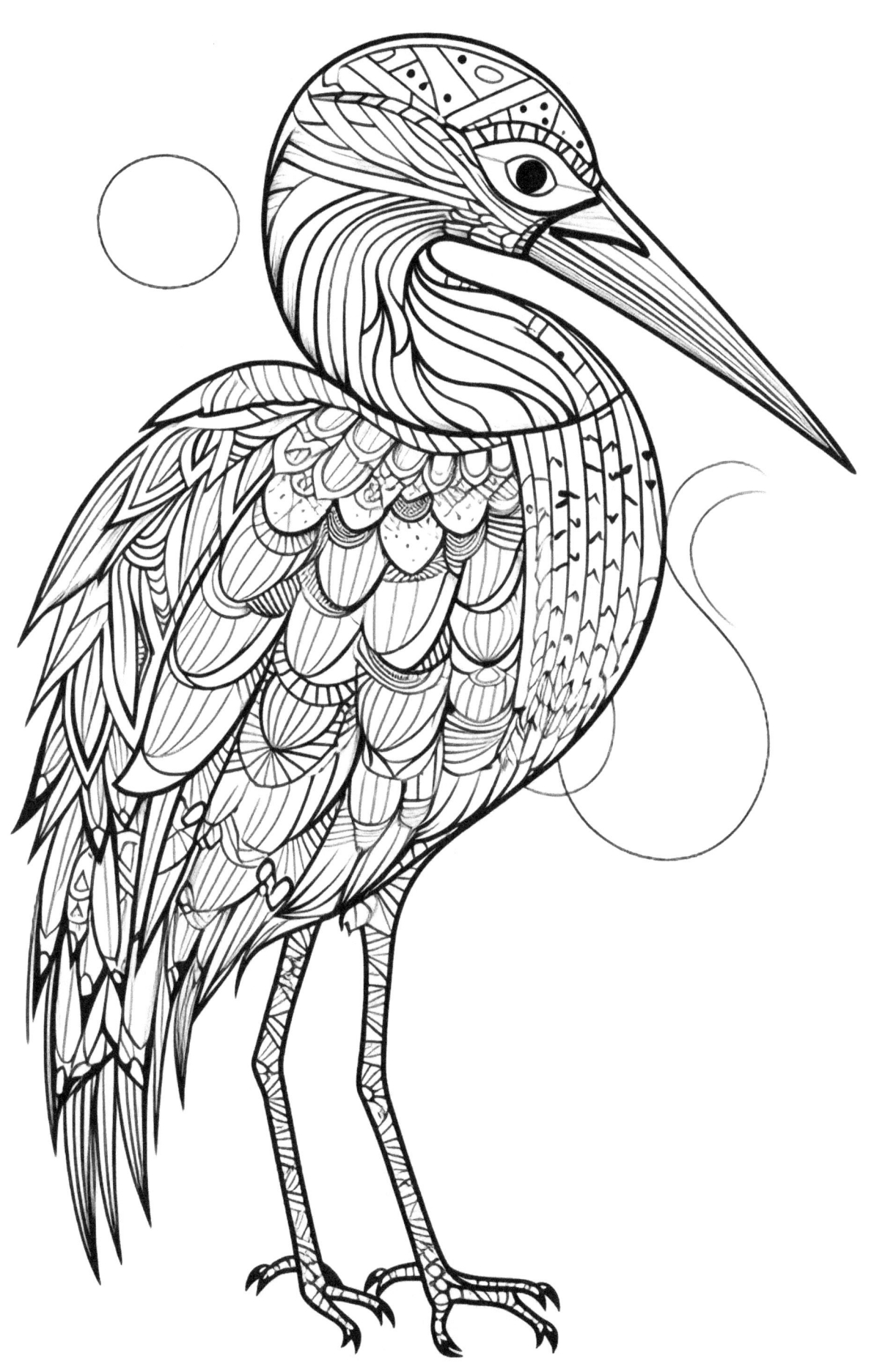

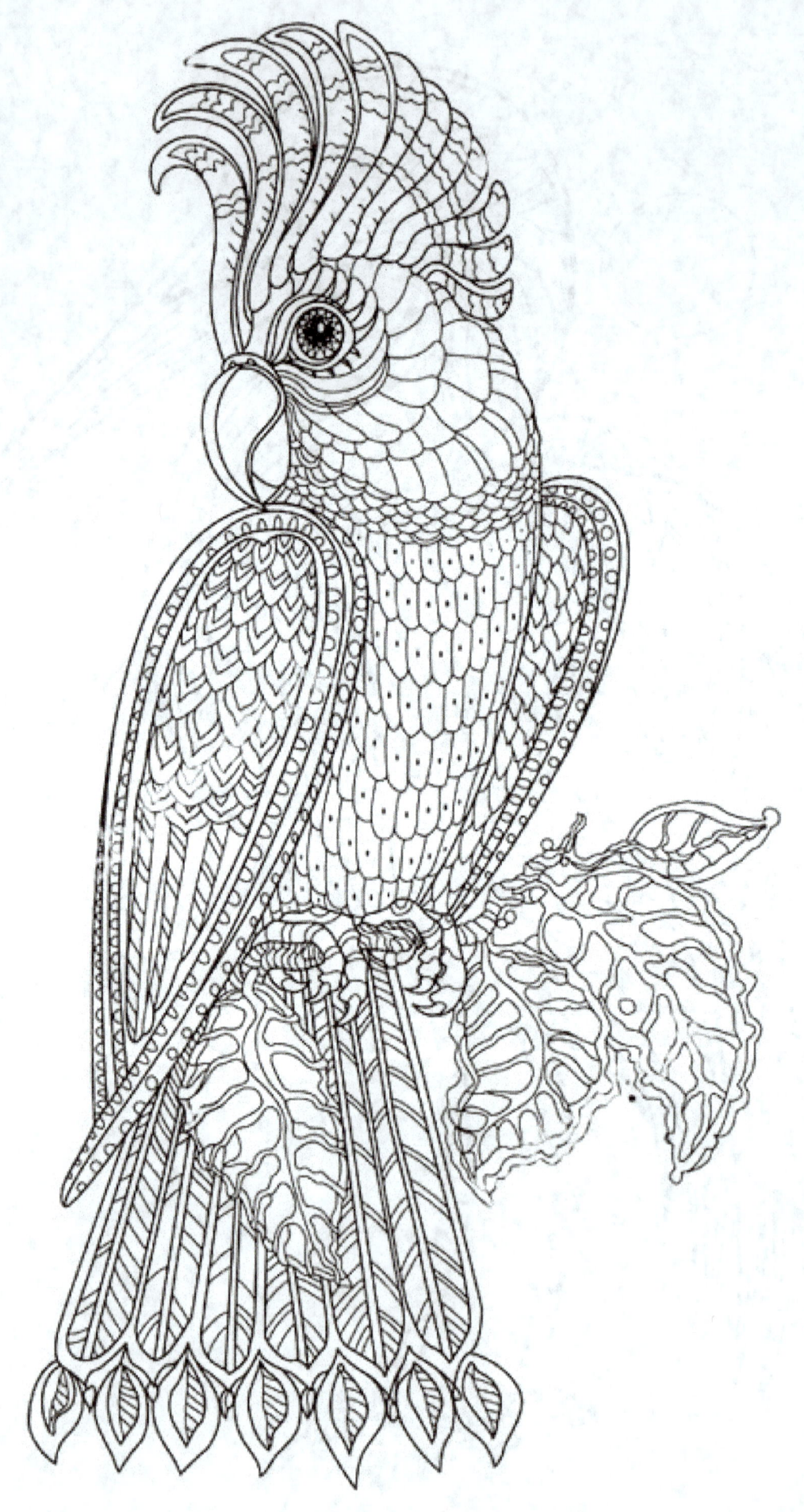

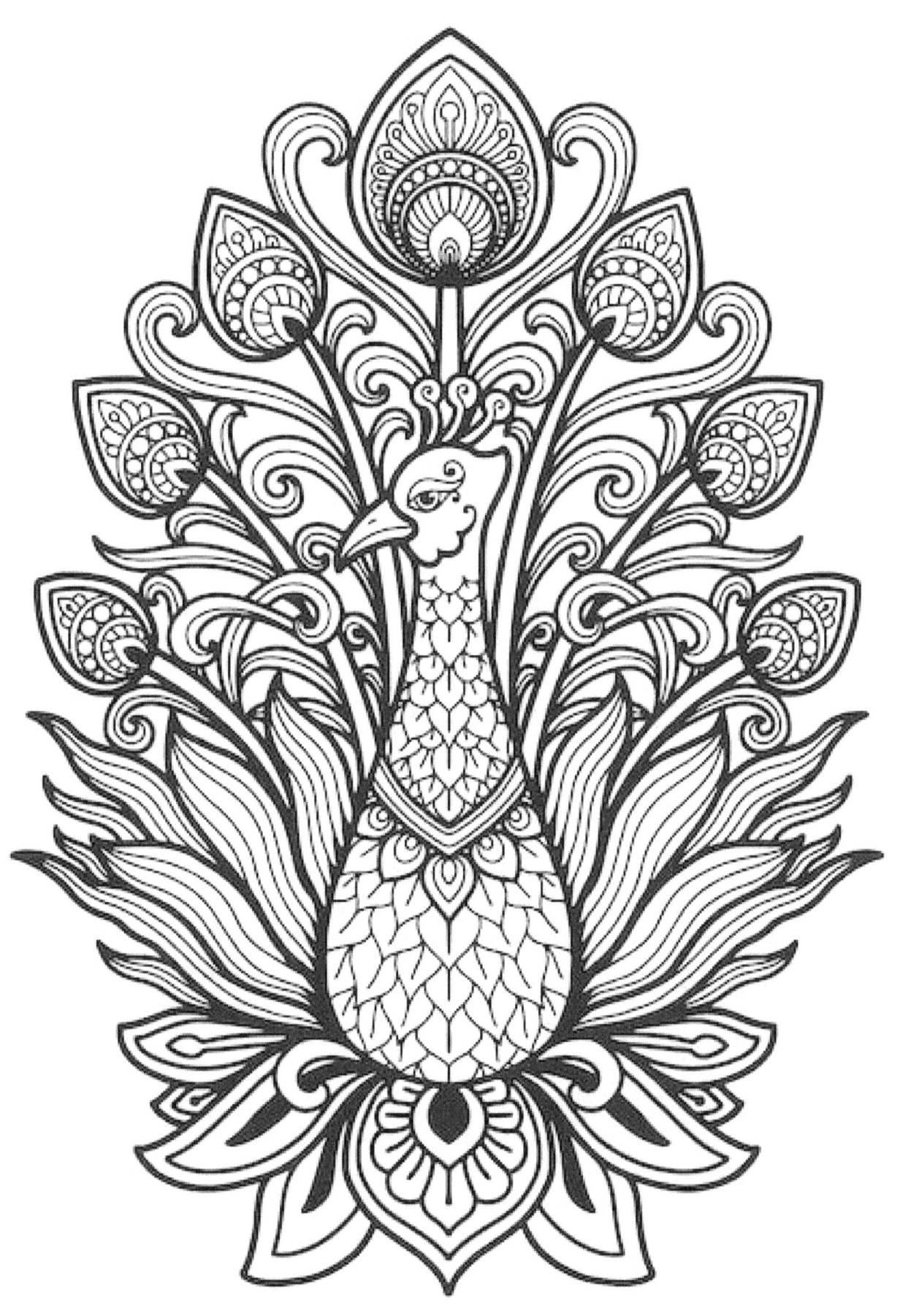

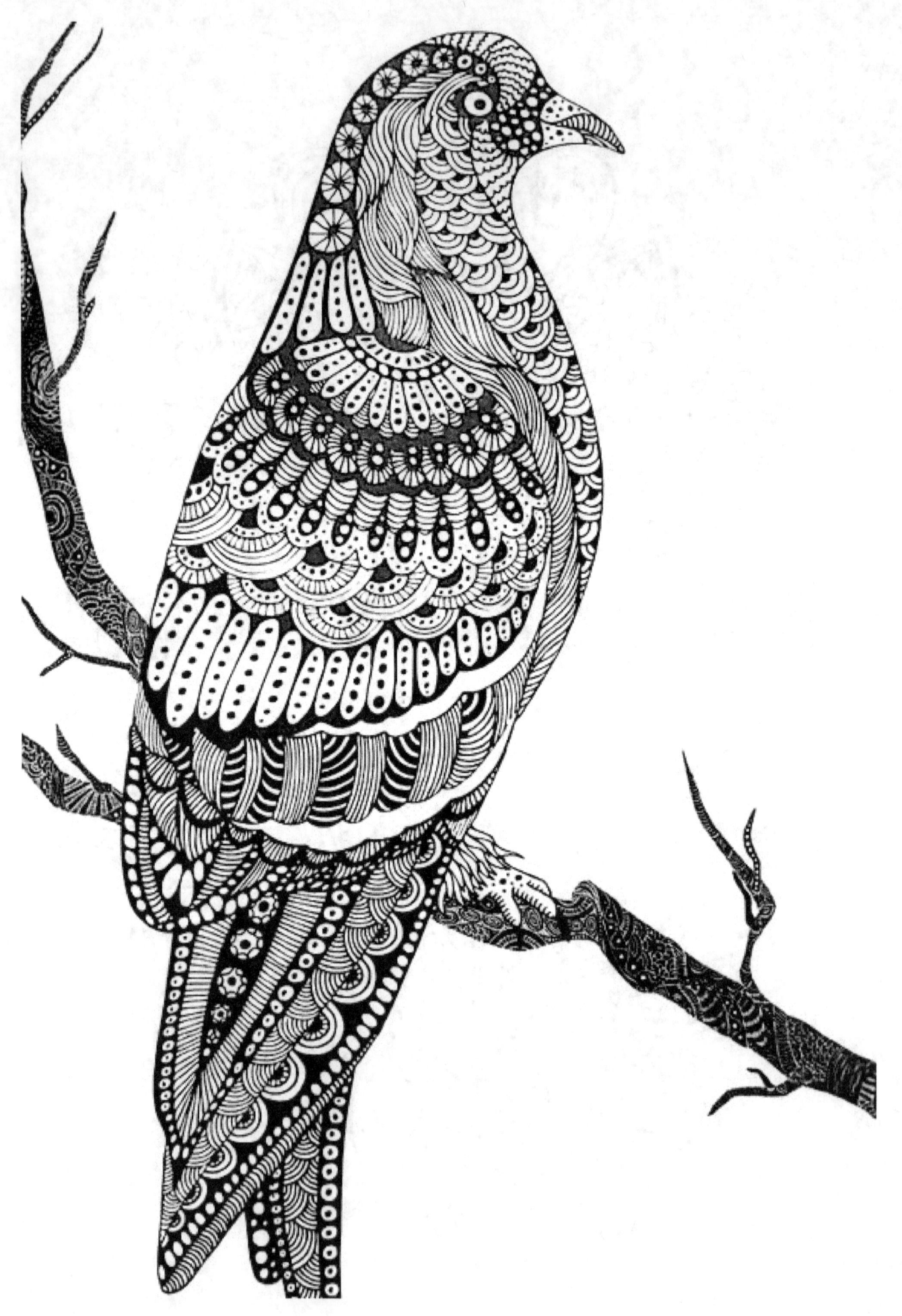

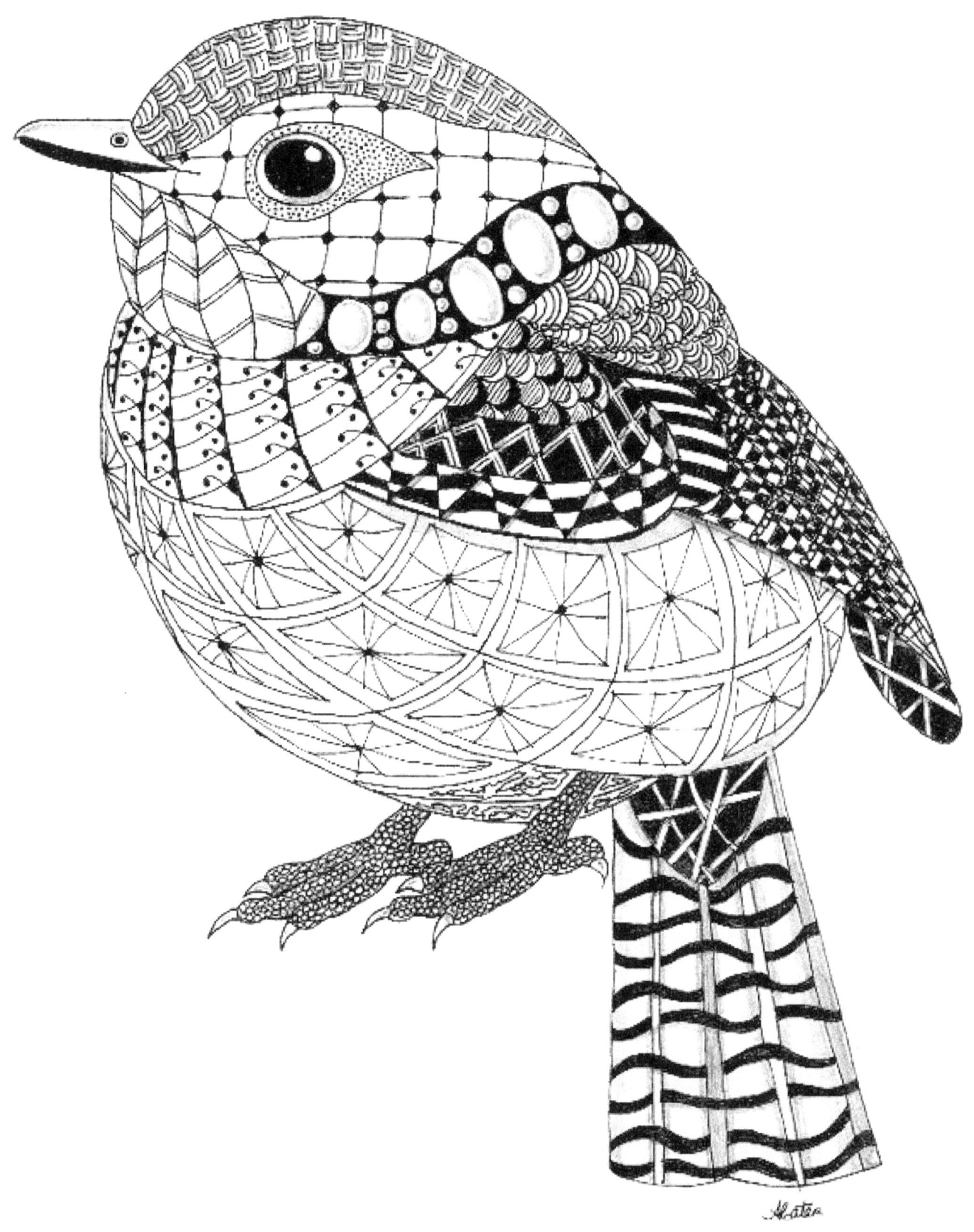

www.ingramcontent.com/pod-product-compliance
Lightning Source LLC
Chambersburg PA
CBHW062232220526
45471CB00009B/3454